RUN
Endure the Pain, Keep the Faith, Finish Your Race

Ferdie Cabiling
with Walter Walker

Few people will ever run across the Philippines, which is exactly why Pastor Ferdie is a unique man and a leader of leaders. Take time to read his story and the insights he draws from endurance running.

—DR. FRANK DAMAZIO
Founder, Frank Damazio Ministries

Most adventure books inspire through the heroics of human self-preservation. *Run* inspires us with something deeper, more purposeful, and more long-lasting—heroics for the sake of others. The Running Pastor does not flinch in showing his weakness, pain, passion, or humanity while asking us "Who are you a champion for?" *Run* is a page-turning energy drink for the soul.

—DR. DAVE WARD
Professor of Homiletics, Indiana Wesleyan University

This book is a must-read for everyone who wants to start strong and finish well in their life's race. Bishop Ferdie Cabiling, or as many call him, the Running Pastor, knows how to endure the pain, stay in the game, and finish the race as an experienced runner. Ferdie inspires all of us to run our races until the "finish line" of our lives. The strong biblical principles outlined and told in the book will inspire and motivate readers to be joyful in times of painful experiences, to keep the faith in the midst of a faithless world, and to finish the race even as many have withdrawn from the challenging course.

—BISHOP NOEL PANTOJA
National Director, Philippine Council of Evangelical Churches

The essence of Pastor Ferdie, I think, is his way of doing life. He demonstrates excellence in all his life roles—as a husband to Judy, a father to Elle and Philip, a leader at Victory, and a proclaimer of God's Word. He is laser-focused, courageous, and continues to pay the price to equip and build the next generation of leaders, for which we are so grateful.

—RACHEL ONG
Founder and Chief Executive, ROHEI

When Pastor Ferdie told me he was going to run across the Philippines to raise funds for the scholars of the Real LIFE Foundation, I thought he was crazy. But knowing what a passionate, disciplined, and committed leader he is, I trusted that if anyone could do it, he could. Pastor Ferdie truly lives out what it means to "run with endurance the race set before us." Our Real LIFE scholars were so amazed that anyone would endure such hardship and physical pain to support their dreams to get an education and a better future, and it inspired them to also "finish strong." *Run* will challenge you to identify the "race" God has set out for you and to run in a way that will honor God and serve others.

—LYNN NAWATA
Asia Pacific Director, Day2 International
Executive Director, Real LIFE Foundation (2008-2016)

There are two passions that Ferdie (a bishop of Victory) and I (a Catholic priest) share: preaching the gospel and ultra-long-distance running. This inspiring book is based on his epic run across the Philippines and the life lessons drawn from it. It not only tells the story about the journey on his feet, but also his life's journey—a journey of faith. With the Apostle Paul, he can truly say: ". . . I have run the full distance, and I have kept the faith." (2 Timothy 4:7, GNT)

—FR. AMADO "PICX" L. PICARDAL, CSSR
Redemptorist Church in Baclaran, Parañaque
Fifth to run across the Philippines (Davao to Aparri, 2011)

The Christian life is often referred to as a race. As followers of Jesus, we are called to fix our eyes on Him, persevere, and fight the good fight of faith. In this book, Ferdie passionately shares his journey with the Lord and in ministry through the lens of his experience as a runner. It contains valuable lessons for all who desire to finish the race well. May the wisdom found in this book encourage all to press on and serve Jesus faithfully until the end.

—DR. PETER TAN-CHI
Senior Pastor, Christ's Commission Fellowship

What a captivating book of faith! *Run* is very encouraging and uplifting, and is definitely an interesting read about a dedicated evangelist's passion for the sport of long-distance running—for a cause. Ferdie's sheer determination and focus toward his end goal captivate my adventurous spirit and inspire me to do great exploits for God and His people as well. His pursuing love for his Lord and Savior and for the scholars of the Real LIFE Foundation is a story of God's love manifesting in and through this great man of God. Well done, Pastor Ferdie.

—DALE ABENOJAR
First Filipino to climb Mt. Everest
(March 14, 2006, 10:45 a.m. Beijing time)
Founder and Missionary Evangelist
Gospel Expedition Ministries, Inc.

On my first glance of Ferdie, I thought he had the look to become a transnational runner. Still, during our initial meeting, I reminded him to check his inner purpose for doing *RUN50*. I realized he had enough of it, and I had no doubt he would certainly accomplish the run as planned.

—CESAR GUARIN
Global Runner

Ferdie Cabiling inspires me. In his run across the Philippines, in his pursuit of a life of purpose, he stirs us and then he coaches us to our best. I am changed by how he lives and what he writes. You will be too.

—DR. STEPHEN MANSFIELD
New York Times Best-selling Author

Bishop Ferdie writes: "When God stirs your heart and gives you a dream, He'll provide the grace to believe it, embrace it, and complete it." These words not only sum up how my own cross-country runs came to be, they also remind us to never stop making the impossible happen.

—JOY ROJAS
Writer, Editor, Long-distance Runner
(Davao to Pagudpud, 2005; California to New York, 2009)

Run is the amazing real-life story of the Running Pastor who did what no one else has done. Bishop Ferdie Cabiling ran from the southernmost tip to the northernmost point of the Philippines, a total of 2,180 km in 44 days.

Filled with rich and practical lessons, this moving account of his less than 50-day marathon retells his life's journey from obscurity to significance, punctuated by his conversion at age 19 and immediate involvement in Christian ministry. You will also learn more about his church, Victory, its members, and their all-out support and participation in this historic run.

Bishop Ferdie Cabiling has become a world-class athlete through many years of discipline and determination, careful planning and proper conditioning, and the pursuit of a godly purpose. His life demonstrates what it means to endure the pain, keep the faith, and finish your race. He is a present-day hero of our faith.

His achievement is the fruit of his complete surrender to the Lord Jesus, obedience to the Word, and resolve to glorify the Almighty God.

—BISHOP EFRAIM TENDERO
Secretary General, World Evangelical Alliance

Do you need a massive dose of inspiration to keep running the race? This amazing book will speak God's Word and power into your situation.

—BO SANCHEZ
Best-selling Author

The book has helped me to further understand how God moves in the different areas of our life: in each race we take on, in each triumph we celebrate, and in each struggle we face. More importantly, I realized how vital it is to dream; to allow myself to see through God's eyes without limiting the possibilities according to my capabilities.

—MATTHEW IRVIN MARLOU AQUINO
Center/Power Forward (Jersey No. 13), National University

We must all see beyond the surface of events and characters until we find God's purpose. When the Running Pastor first shared his plan to run across the Philippines, most people thought in terms of logistics, challenges, and the attention that a Running Pastor might attract. But once his feet were up and running, when the aches and pains and blisters started to build up, when cheering squads and encouragement started spreading thin by virtue of terrain and islands separating everyone, I know that what kept the Running Pastor going was his love for God, his passion to share God with others, and knowing that on the finish line his family would be waiting with arms wide open, ready to refill all the love he gave out all across the country. May the stories herein ignite your passion, especially your love for God.

—CITO BELTRAN
Columnist and Opinion Writer, *The Philippine Star*

Ferdie Cabiling is a true hero. His courageous life is an inspiration to me and thousands more. Dare to follow his incredible journey through the pages of this book—you will be compelled to action. He demonstrates that the gospel is the cure for injustice and evil and should be heard by everyone everywhere.

—DR. RICE BROOCKS
Cofounder, Every Nation
Author of *God's Not Dead* and *The Human Right*

RUN

**ENDURE THE PAIN,
KEEP THE FAITH,
FINISH YOUR RACE**

FERDIE CABILING
WITH WALTER WALKER

Run
Endure the Pain, Keep the Faith, Finish Your Race
Copyright © 2018 by Ferdie Cabiling
All rights reserved

Unless otherwise noted, Scripture quotations are from the English Standard Version, Copyright © 2001 by Crossway, a publishing ministry of Good News Publishers. Used by permission. All rights reserved.

Scripture quotations marked NASB are taken from The Holy Bible, the New American Standard Bible® (NASB), Copyright © 1960, 1962, 1963, 1968, 1971, 1972, 1973,1975, 1977, 1995 by The Lockman Foundation. Used by permission. www.Lockman.org

Scripture quotations marked NIV are taken from The Holy Bible, New International Version®, NIV® Copyright ©1973, 1978, 1984, 2011 by Biblica, Inc®. Used by permission. All rights reserved worldwide.

No part of this book may be used or reproduced in any manner, whatsoever, without any written permission, except in the case of brief quotations clearly cited.

For more information on sales, licensing, or permissions, contact the publisher:

Every Nation Resources
P.O. Box 1787
Brentwood, TN 37024-1787

Trade Paperback ISBN: 978-179-699-154-3

Printed in The United States of America

Dedication

Before I ran across the Philippines, my wife, Judy, and her friends had a conversation about my run. The women expressed their concerns and asked, "Aren't you worried about your husband doing this? He might die! Aren't you worried at all?" Judy simply replied, "Why are you worried? Last time I checked, I'm the wife, and I'm not worried."

Judy is a woman of courage and confidence, and she never fails to inspire me as I unintentionally drag her into my crazy ideas and adventures. She has always been a strong support to me and our family. I feel ready to conquer the world when she is beside me.

As we were preparing for *RUN50*, Judy made things happen. She was the woman behind the logistics of the run. She planned and coordinated with key people across the Philippines. Because of her, we were able to get hundreds of volunteers from our church. She also asked for help from several pastors to coordinate with local government units and running clubs. She's the person who looked for people who connected us to the Body of Christ in key locations and forged partnerships with nongovernmental organizations such as Operation Blessing. Judy has always been steps ahead of others in life and paves the way for people to follow.

As the African proverb says, "If you want to go fast, go alone. If you want to go far, go together." As I look back at the marathons I joined and even at this race called life, I am grateful to God for providing a faithful partner who has been by my side. Running across the Philippines and raising a godly family would not have been possible without her. She is one of the expressions of God's grace in my life. I know that there is still a long way ahead of us, but I am confident to face it knowing she is with me.

Judy, thank you for being a wife to me and a mother to our children. Thank you for your love for Jesus and for your devotion to His kingdom. This book is dedicated to you.

Contents

Acknowledgments

Foreword

Follow the *RUN50* Route

ENDURE THE PAIN
1. RUN50
   Lessons for the Long Run 1
2. Tough Growing
   Why I Am the Way I Am..7
3. Starting Line
   The Beginning of Another Race 17
4. Basic Training
   Growing as You're Going...29
5. Champion-ship
   The Practice of Standing in the Gap...39
6. Passion
   Running for Those Who Can't Run for Themselves...............49

KEEP THE FAITH
7. Preparation
   Building the Case for the Hope that is in You..........................65
8. Your Race
   Running for Your Life 79
9. Your Calling
   The Race that is Set before You 89
10. Your Focus
    Fixing Your Eyes on Jesus...99
11. Your Vision
    Keeping Pace with an Expanding Stewardship 105
12. Your Faith
    Learning from Your Heroes 113

FINISH YOUR RACE

13. Your Audience
    Running for the One Who is Watching 129
14. Your Finish
    Looking Back at What You've Learned 141

Epilogue

References

About the Author

Acknowledgments

I want to express my heartfelt appreciation to the Victory pastors, churches, and other personnel who helped me along the way.

Nowell Evangelista of Victory General Santos, together with Michael Chiongbian, was very sensitive to my needs. He's a great leader who set the pace for other pastors to follow during *RUN50*.

Alvin Supan of Victory Davao, together with his wife, Vicky, are old friends of ours from back in Manila. Their eldest son, Josh, is our godchild. They welcomed us warmly and celebrated my 50th birthday in Davao on the fourth day of *RUN50*. It was like a family celebration.

Joseph Doce and Tom Arellano of Victory Tagum, along with their friends, enthusiastically supported us by meeting all our needs.

On the day I reached Butuan City, Noel Agcaoili of Victory Butuan had just arrived from London after attending his sister's wedding. In spite of jet lag and not having seen his family for weeks, he sacrificially worked as my driver and crew at the same time. His wife, Chay, and daughter, Summer, accompanied him and became my photographers. When my foot was injured, Noel acted as my physical therapist as well, massaging my feet and legs to ease the pain. He witnessed my difficulty in running to the end of Mindanao.

Kix Javier of Victory Tacloban and his wife, Bless, collaborated with Mayor Alfred Romualdez to provide everything I needed for *RUN50*. Kix assisted me during the Leyte and Samar runs; Mayor Romualdez supported us in so many ways; he provided us with a van, an ambulance, and a speedboat at the end of our run through Mindanao.

A team of pastors and leaders from Cebu, led by Raymund Cañete, helped cover the entire island of Leyte as runners, pacers, and support crew.

Alan Lopez of Victory Sorsogon is a doctor and pastor—*RUN50* is my second collaborative run with him. He knew me well enough to head the team in Sorsogon City during the run. I felt so at home there because of their team.

Al Bantayan of Victory Legazpi stayed with me from Sorsogon to Naga City during the run to show his support.

Jason Calara and his wife, Mary Jane, were nurses in the United Kingdom but returned to the Philippines to plant a church in Naga. During *RUN50*, I was able to preach at the launch of Victory Naga.

Ed Ty of Victory Lucena was a longtime pastor in the province whose strong connections enabled me to pray for four leading officials during our run through Quezon. He and his team served me until I reached Metro Manila.

Ariel Marquez of Victory Alabang and his wife, Shirley, are our old friends and neighbors. He and his team ran with us on our way to Muntinlupa.

Rouie Gutierrez, Erick Fernandez, Rizal Padrique, Loyd Janobas, and Anthony Licud of Victory churches in Bulacan joined forces to show support for *RUN50*, and their enthusiasm to do things together created a "fiesta feel" the whole time I was running through the Bulacan area.

Arnold Pascual of Victory Cabanatuan and his staff rallied the local runners and joined me in the run.

Jerome Gutierrez of Victory City of San Fernando, who leads the Victory churches in Central Luzon, rode his motorbike to Bulacan and joined the festivities. Together with the pastors of Central Luzon, Jerome made a generous contribution to the Real LIFE Foundation.

Romar Flores of Victory Bayombong and his wife, Chicklet, are both runners. They earnestly prepared for *RUN50* months before the actual run. The day I ran in Nueva Vizcaya, the province was placed under public storm warning signal number 3. Romar, Chicklet, and their team bravely continued the run with me in the pouring rain. Their dedication and faith were amazing.

Jay Medrano of Victory Cauayan is a young pastor who supported us by organizing local runners and providing lunch for our team.

Julius Vaquilar of Victory Santiago was one of those originally reached in Victory Baguio. He is a nurse and local politician, married to Beth, a doctor. Julius ran with me until he could run no more, then rode his scooter just to be a part of the team. Julius is a born comedian.

Together with his entire family, Jude Lingan of Victory Ilagan organized the whole church to support *RUN50* and prepared a big lunch for everyone.

Ross Resuello of Victory Tuguegarao was an original campus missionary from the 1980s. Along with his wife, Mona, he is one of the longest-serving pastors in the province. Ross is also a local politician and has a business that provides jobs to hundreds of locals. He organized a grand welcome for me and mobilized the whole church and town—including the mayor—to participate in the run. It was indeed a grand ending for *RUN50*.

Thanks to Elisa Yu and Layla Lopez who served as the administrators of *RUN50*.

The 2015 Real LIFE Foundation team, led by Lynn Nawata, made it easier for us to raise support for the scholars.

Operation Blessing, Dr. Kim Pascual, Mr. and Mrs. Arnold and Nimfa Petel, and Jerome Lagueras stepped in and assisted during *RUN50* in Mindanao's most dangerous places.

Steve Cadd and Joseph Landreth-Smith volunteered to document *RUN50* for free and made a 10-minute film.

Dyan Castillejo featured *RUN50* in her sports segment twice, and the run was broadcasted throughout the Philippines. As I ran, people recognized me because of that interview.

My pacers' and running buddies' energy and funny stories provided the encouragement I needed to complete *RUN50*.

Varsha Daswani, Jaret Garcia, Esther Suson, and the Communications and Technology Department of Every Nation Philippines helped produce this book.

My daughter, Elizabeth, escorted me to the starting point in General Santos City, was with me in the middle in Tacloban City, and ran hand in hand with me to the *RUN50* finish.

My wife Judy has been my partner, my encourager, and the love of my life for 27 years. Walter Walker was the campus pastor of Dr. Rice Broocks and Pastor Steve Murrell at Mississippi State University. These two came to Manila in 1984 and imparted to us what they had received from Walter (2 Timothy 2:2). Walter and Judy worked with me for countless hours extracting stories, reflections, and comments on my run across the Philippines. Without them this manuscript would never have been written.

The Philippine National Police helped bring extra security and needed protection in almost all the towns I passed via the Pan-Philippine Highway.

So many others supported and participated in *RUN50* that it would be impossible to thank them all. Over 500 contributed in one way or another, and that's not even counting the 415 donors who gave to support Real LIFE Foundation scholars. I've been deeply moved by everyone's sacrifice and all-out support for us as co-laborers in the Lord and for *RUN50's* goal of raising funds for the scholars. Many thanks to you all!

Foreword

In June of 1984, when I first met Ferdie Cabiling, I was a 25-year-old clueless church planter with a full head of hair, and he was a timid 19-year-old engineering student responding to the gospel. Today, more than three decades later, I no longer have hair, and he is no longer timid.

For those who know him now, it might be difficult to imagine Ferdie ever being timid. But here's how timid he was. That first night we met after an evangelistic meeting at the Girl Scouts of the Philippines Auditorium, I thought he said his name was "Freddy." After calling him Freddy for almost three weeks, he finally sheepishly corrected me and told me his name was Ferdie. Whether you know him as Ferdie, Kuya Ferdie, Coach Ferdie, Pastor Ferdie, Bishop Ferdie, or "Freddy," you will be glad you read this book.

While reading through the first draft of the manuscript, several thoughts quickly came to mind.

The first thing is perhaps the most obvious. There has always been a side of Ferdie that's just a little bit crazy, extreme, and over-the-top in everything I've ever known him to do. We've all seen it in the way he preaches, prays, and serves, and in his commitment to following Christ, making disciples, and running. He's also been a loyal friend for most of my adult life.

That being said, my 34-year friendship and ministry partnership with Ferdie is kind of an enigma. How is it that someone as laid back as me has felt so comfortable for so long with a hyper-aggressive leader like Ferdie Cabiling? Through the years, I've known quite a few obsessively intense leaders. Over time, their passion and persistence tends to just wear out the introverts around them. But I've never felt that way with Ferdie, and I've often wondered why. Though we learned to admire and celebrate our differences long ago, there's a revealing aspect of Ferdie's story particularly highlighted in this book. It has enabled me to put my finger on the reason he is such a great leader and why we have been able to work well together for over three decades.

It's really quite simple if you think about it. He doesn't compare the race before him with the races others are called to run. While he's an eternal optimist and persistent encourager, he allows others to run at their own pace. And he can celebrate the completion of his physically-challenged son's lap around the neighborhood with the same enthusiasm as a finish in the infamous *Bataan Death March 160K Ultra Marathon Race*. Ferdie simply runs his own race with his eyes fixed and focused on Jesus, the author and perfecter of his faith. For Ferdie, it's never about beating or out-performing anyone else. It's always about honoring God and running together.

I was out of the country during *RUN50*, and I couldn't make an appearance until the last day. I had been tracking his progress—reading blogs, watching the podcasts, and talking to people on the phone. On the 43rd day, the eve of his final 50-km run to the finish line, I arrived in time for a short visit with the now-famous Running Pastor.

Both of us were raised in the tradition of the "stiff upper lip." Our fathers made sure that we understood that boys don't cry. I'm not sure what it was, maybe something in the air, but during our visit, we were both having a difficult time controlling our "sweating eyes." Perhaps being a witness to the last day's run inspired the former runner in me. Of course, I never ran a race farther than 200 meters. Nevertheless, there's something profoundly inspirational about a competitor finishing a race like this with such uncommon determination and endurance. It's the kind of thing that will cause a great cloud of witnesses to watch intently and cheer wildly. More than the former runner in me, it was the Christ-follower in me that was far more affected.

Even more than that, in *Run: Endure the Pain, Keep the Faith, Finish Your Race,* Ferdie articulates a most profound understanding of what it means to champion the cause of those in need. *RUN50* raised over PHP 2 million for Real LIFE Foundation scholars. "Champion-ship," as Ferdie calls it, is essential to our understanding of discipleship. Through a series of intensely personal stories, Ferdie progressively unpacks four levels of following Christ based on how we champion the cause of those we serve. If you take nothing else away from the book, those insights will challenge your understanding of what it really means to be a disciple.

Finally, in the second half of the book, Ferdie relates his experiences as an ultramarathoner to the struggles of a small group of weary believers in the early church—the recipients of the epistle to the Hebrews. Phrase by phrase, he breaks down the exhortation of Hebrews 12:1,2:

> Therefore, since we are surrounded by so great a cloud of witnesses, let us also lay aside every weight, and sin which clings so closely, and let us run with endurance the race that is set before us, looking to Jesus, the founder and perfecter of our faith, who for the joy that was set before him endured the cross, despising the shame, and is seated at the right hand of the throne of God.

I have frequently heard writers and preachers refer to that passage, but I've never heard or read such thorough and meaningful applications. If anyone ever had anything profound to say about running with endurance the race set before you, it would be Ferdie Cabiling—the Running Pastor. And he says it as well as I have ever heard it said.

As I pursue the particular race God has set before me, Ferdie has always been one of my primary spiritual pacers, and I measure my passion and my dedication by the pace he sets.

Thanks, Ferdie, for this book and the example you set for us all.

—STEVE MURRELL
Founding Pastor, Victory
Cofounder and President, Every Nation Churches & Ministries

Follow the RUN 50 Route

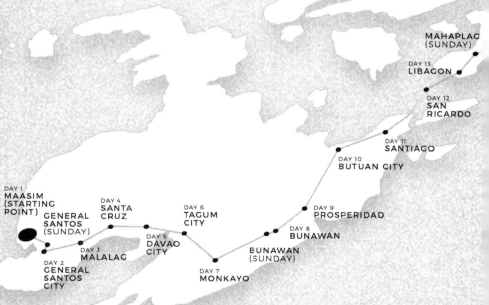

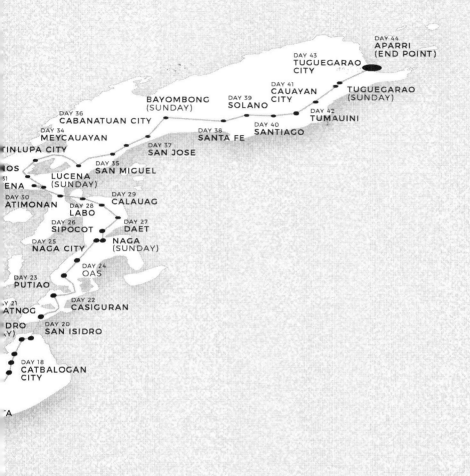

ENDURE THE PAIN

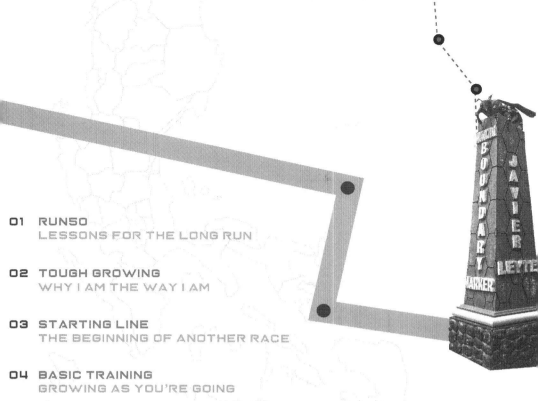

01 RUN50
LESSONS FOR THE LONG RUN

02 TOUGH GROWING
WHY I AM THE WAY I AM

03 STARTING LINE
THE BEGINNING OF ANOTHER RACE

04 BASIC TRAINING
GROWING AS YOU'RE GOING

05 CHAMPION-SHIP
THE PRACTICE OF STANDING IN THE GAP

06 PASSION
RUNNING FOR THOSE WHO CAN'T RUN
FOR THEMSELVES

01
RUN50
LESSONS FOR THE LONG RUN

God made me fast. And when I run, I feel His pleasure.

ERIC LIDDELL
1924 Paris Olympics, Gold Medalist, 400 m
Missionary to China

Have you not known? Have you not heard?
The Lord is the everlasting God,
the Creator of the ends of the earth.

He does not faint or grow weary;
his understanding is unsearchable.
He gives power to the faint,
and to him who has no might he increases strength.

Even youths shall faint and be weary,
and young men shall fall exhausted;
but they who wait for the Lord shall renew their strength;
they shall mount up with wings like eagles;
they shall run and not be weary;
they shall walk and not faint.

ISAIAH 40:28-31

On September 5, 2015, in the province of Sarangani at the municipality of Maasim, 57.5 kilometers (km) south of General Santos City by road, on the southern tip of the southernmost province of the Philippines, I set out on a 2,180-km run across the Philippine Islands. I ran with a team of volunteer pacers from our church who took turns pacing me in 20- to 50-km segments—keeping me focused, encouraged, and (most of the time) on course.

There were also teams of drivers, organizers, and running clubs from all over the Philippines who joined in at various stretches along the way. In all, over 500 volunteers participated in one way or another.

The course was laid out in 44 stages, daily runs of approximately 50 km that began each day at around 2:00 a.m. With the aid of my Garmin Forerunner 920XT watch and the Runkeeper running app as backup, I measured run times and distances for each segment. Many days, we'd end the run in a city. Occasionally, I'd just run until my Garmin hit 50 km. Then we'd drive to the nearest town or village and return to the same spot at about 2:00 a.m. the next day to begin another 50-km run. The pacers and I ran six days each week for over seven weeks, taking Sundays off so I could preach in churches along the way. During those 44 days, I celebrated my 50th birthday. Consequently, this transnational run came to be known as *RUN50*.

Running through the provinces from south to north was not without its hazards. Day 6 and Day 7 took us through one of the most dangerous regions of the Philippines. Police officers from Tagum City, Monkayo, and Bunawan escorted us through those sections of Mindanao. On Day 6, I began the day's run at 1:00 a.m., running alone with the crew and the officers in their vehicles. We were still running in those dangerous areas the following day. At one point on the road from Montevista up to Bunawan, I stopped at the top of a hill to talk with my crew. Suddenly, police officers with rifles poured out of their van and came toward us.

"Sir, please do not stop here," an officer said. "You can talk more at the bottom of this slope but not here. A Philippine Army colonel was ambushed on this very spot!"

The decision to run across the Philippines was the latest in a lifetime of self-imposed running challenges, beginning in my college days at Adamson University. All of my early runs were recreational, my first official race being the *10-km Nike+ Human Race* in 2008.

Four years later, in 2011, I stepped my running up to another level when I was introduced to ultramarathon races—runs of 42 km or more. My first was the *Tagaytay to Nasugbu 50K Ultra Marathon Race* in November 2010. The next year I doubled the distance at the *Bataan Death March 102K Ultra Marathon Race*. Over the next four years, I entered many other ultra-long races with running mates from Victory, our church. An exhausting three-stage run in the *Bataan Death March 160K Ultra Marathon Race* in 2012 left me so mentally and physically depleted, I even contemplated ending my participation in ultramarathons. I do not say end my "career" because I'm not a professional runner. I'm a pastor, called and committed to preaching the gospel and making disciples. And to that purpose, there's no slowing down, no retiring, no quitting.

While still trying to recover from that three-stage 160-km run, the Lord planted an idea in my heart that was larger than anything I had ever considered. The result was that I locked in on the vision for *RUN50*. In the *160-km Bataan Death March* in 2012, I had run a little over 50 km in each of the three stages. The 2,180-km run across the Philippines would be a quantum leap forward as a runner that would take three more years of training and preparation.

On Monday, October 26, 2015, less than 50 days after it began, I completed the last leg of *RUN50*—beginning at Maasim, Sarangani, and crossing the finish line at Aparri, Cagayan, at the northernmost edge of the island of Luzon. My team of pacers and I had each recruited financial partners in support of Real LIFE Foundation, a Philippine nongovernment organization with the vision of transforming lives, families, and communities through hope and education.

The promotional impact was quite remarkable. One of the largest television networks in the Philippines provided primetime coverage of *RUN50* and Real LIFE Foundation. Local reporters and members of the media interviewed me and published stories along the way. Daily online updates and videos were posted on websites, including those of Real LIFE and Victory. I had the privilege of meeting with dozens of mayors and hundreds of city officials, sharing both the story of the Real LIFE Foundation scholars and the greatest story of all—the gospel of Jesus Christ. In addition to raising awareness, by the completion of *RUN50*, 415 donors had given PHP 2,885,482.00 to the Real LIFE Foundation.

In short, that's the story of *RUN50*, but there was so much more that happened and so much more that I learned in the process.

LESSONS LEARNED ALONG THE WAY

I truly enjoyed the encouragement and companionship of my pacers, my support team, and the volunteer runners who joined me at various times throughout the run. There were also times during *RUN50* that I ran alone. By "alone," I mean with a van full of security forces carrying assault rifles trailing me through some of the most dangerous parts of the Philippines. To the extent that I was alone, it gave me the opportunity to think—mostly about those running with me, those I was running for, and about the One for Whom we were ultimately running. As I ran, I learned many things—personal lessons that I hope you will take away from the *RUN50* story.

Firstly, I learned to remain focused on what I had been called to do—the race set before me. Running ultramarathons can be extremely boring, but a transnational run across the Philippines? Boring times 50. Some runners quit a race because they're tired or injured. Others quit from boredom rather than from fatigue. Being a successful ultramarathoner requires a lot of mental energy. As one gets accustomed to the distances, running becomes like aerobic meditation. You quit thinking about running and just think about thinking. That's delightful for some, torturous for others, depending on what thoughts come up during the hours and days of a long run. Consequently, you'd better have a deep reservoir of thoughts that inspire, excite, and challenge you. The ideas that you allow to run through your head either empower you or drain you. In J. M. Barrie's classic story, *Peter Pan*, Peter empowers the Darling children to fly by teaching them to focus on their happy thoughts. It's much like the Apostle Paul's admonition to his beloved church in Philippi: "Whatever is true, whatever is honorable, whatever is just, whatever is pure, whatever is lovely, whatever is commendable, if there is any excellence, if there is anything worthy of praise, think about these things" (Philippians 4:8, NRSV). Training for ultramarathons requires mental as well as physical discipline. Running with endurance the race God has set before us—even more so.

Secondly, I learned about championing the cause of those in need—running for those who cannot run for themselves. Some of you know our son, Philip. Seeing him run his particular race continues to be both an inspiration and lesson to me on what it means to follow Christ as the champion of our salvation. That's why, in the following pages, I have a few things to say about running with and on behalf of others.

Thirdly, through all those years of running, and particularly during the training and execution of *RUN50*, I learned a lot about focus and vision, purpose and passion, and perseverance and endurance. With that in mind, the epistle to the Hebrews has become quite meaningful to me. The epistle seems to be an exhortation to a small group of Jewish believers within the larger Christian community—to those who, in the face of persecution, were contemplating shrinking back from following Christ. Throughout the epistle, the author was urging them to run with endurance the race set before them. In the second half of this book, I have a few things to say about these believers and the challenges they faced.

Fourthly, during the preparation stage of *RUN50*, I learned that while a great dream is initially exhilarating, it's never fulfilled without seasons of great testing. Such dreams and visions do not come without many critics and detractors. Like the opponents of Nehemiah's audacious vision to restore the walls of Jerusalem, naysayers will discourage you, ridicule you, or dismiss you from pursuing what God has put in your heart. The good news is that you don't need people's permission to dream. When God stirs your heart and gives you a dream, He'll provide the grace to believe it, embrace it, and complete it. He will in time also assign others to encourage you, help you, and share in the victory celebration. Therefore, we'll look at locking in on the vision for the unique race that is set before you and running with relentless endurance.

Lastly, I've had the opportunity to think a lot about those whom I've been called to serve with in Victory. What has happened in our movement over the last three decades greatly exceeds what any of us could ever have hoped for, even in our wildest imaginations. Together we've been entrusted with a stewardship that can be described as both extraordinarily wonderful and extraordinarily woeful. As King David wrote, "He has done **wonderful** things, His right hand and His holy arm have gained the victory for Him"

(Psalm 98:1, NASB). And as the Apostle Paul wrote, "I am under compulsion; for **woe is me** if I do not preach the gospel. For if I do this voluntarily, I have a reward; but if against my will, I have a **stewardship entrusted** to me" (1 Corinthians 9:16,17). And so, I also have a few thoughts about the stewardship with which we have all been entrusted.

A PECULIAR PASSION

I'm a passionate person who is known to do extreme things—like *RUN50*. So maybe a good place to begin is with some explanation—why I do the things I do and how I became the way I am.

02

TOUGH GROWING
WHY I AM THE WAY I AM

Most people run a race to see who is fastest. I run a race to see who has the most guts.

STEVE PREFONTAINE
Multiple U.S. Record-holder in Middle- and Long-distance Running

He who does not know how to look back at where he came from will never get to his destination.

FILIPINO PROVERB

Another of the disciples said to him, "Lord, let me first go and bury my father." And Jesus said to him, "Follow me, and leave the dead to bury their own dead."

MATTHEW 8:21,22

Whether you're an occasional jogger running 10 km for charity, an ultramarathoner, or running across the nation, there are a few common hazards that may prevent you from finishing your race:

1. Dropping out because you're injured;
2. Quitting because you're tired; or
3. Going off-course because you took a wrong turn.

The first hazard, dropping out of the race due to injury, became a real possibility for me.

On Day 6 of *RUN50*, I reached Tagum City in Mindanao, and my left foot and ankle had begun to swell. By Day 7, I had reached Bunawan, Agusan del Sur, and could feel bursts of extreme pain with every step. My lone pacer, J.R. Macanas, and his friend, James Mascariñas (our driver), saw how slow and difficult every step of the run was becoming. We had covered only 350 km of the 2,180-km run, but no way was I going to drop out. I had made a very public commitment, and a sore foot would not cause me to abandon the race. I applied the ointment given to me by my friend, Dr. Jojo Rivera, and pressed on.

The second hazard, fatigue and exhaustion, piled onto the first. Isn't that the way it usually happens? It's not one difficulty that tempts you to quit your race, it's one thing on top of another on top of another—like an avalanche. On Day 9, we started off from Prosperidad, Agusan del Sur. The topography of the land was so mountainous that it made for a challenging run, even on a good day. With an injury, it became quite difficult. By 3:00 a.m., I was running very slowly. J.R. and James were driving ahead to light the road. Seeing a waiting shed by the roadside, I went in, lay down, put my injured foot up, and fell asleep. I don't know how long I slept. I couldn't force myself to get up and continue.

When J.R. and James realized I was no longer following the car, they looked for me frantically. They retraced the route, but I was nowhere to be found. Finally, J.R. happened to shine a light on the waiting shed and it caught the reflector on my shoe. I was lying almost out of sight. He sat beside me in the dark and waited for me to wake up.

J.R. began to suggest that I take the car for the remainder of that leg of *RUN50*. I don't blame him for tempting me with an easy option to quit. He had seen the difficulty I was having. But I saw how worried he was, so I changed the subject and began asking him to tell me about himself, even pressing him on the fact that he was still single. It helped us both focus on other things.

That was my worst day during all of *RUN50*. Times like these really test a runner's resolve. Nonetheless, I never entertained the thought of quitting. By then, the vision of why I was running was too deeply imprinted in my mind. Successful ultramarathoners train to build up mental endurance as much as their physical stamina. They learn how to deal with moments of mental weakness in which they are tempted to surrender the decades they've invested in their race. Strangely enough, my foot got better as I continued to run.

The third hazard that can cause a runner not to finish the race is veering off the set course and getting lost. That happens to some runners when they're running along and not paying close attention to where they're going. Occasionally, a runner will find his or her way back and eventually complete the race. Having taken a wrong turn and continued for many kilometers in the wrong direction, however, most of those runners never finish. That happened to my team in the *Manila to Baguio 250K Ultra Marathon Race* in 2014. I was running ahead of the required time, but we missed a turn and ran off-course. By the time we realized what had happened, it was too late. We had missed the cut-off time by nine minutes and were disqualified.

THE OBSESSIVE-COMPULSIVE PASTOR

The full-throttle, no-holds-barred, outrageous approach to everything I do is hard for some people to understand—running across the Philippines being only one of those fanatical pursuits. Whether it was lifting weights, running ultramarathons, or following hard after Christ, I seem to be compelled to be all in and go all out. I limit the things I'm willing to invest in, but having decided to follow something or someone, I get obsessed with it. It's been suggested on more than one occasion that there's some unresolved issue or obsessive-compulsive tendency driving me to lock on to ridiculously extreme personal objectives. Those making fun of my "personality disorder" are (I hope) just joking. However, if I were pressed for a serious answer, it would simply be this: the deepest imprint stamped on my personality (call it obsessive-compulsive if you wish) was from my father, Buena Ventura Cabiling. I am the way I am primarily because of the way he was.

My father grew up in Barangay Damula-an in the town of Albuera, Leyte. Life there was pretty simple, the people laid-back, friendly, and extremely hospitable. The region was rich in natural resources but lacking the government educational programs and opportunities. Most worked as fishermen and farmers on meager plots of land. In my father's time and place, those things were all you really needed to know. Consequently, he never made it past the third grade. Whatever there was to learn in those first three grades, he either ignored or forgot. My father never learned to read and never made any efforts in later years to learn. I remember, as a child, my school-teacher mother reading everything for him.

On December 8, 1941, ten hours after the attack on the United States' Pacific Fleet in Pearl Harbor, Japan invaded the Philippines. In his later years, my father began to talk about those times. The combined Filipino and American forces put up a heroic resistance. When my father was 18 years old, he helped the U.S. Army by bringing dead American soldiers down from the mountains into Albuera. The out-gunned and under-supplied Americans in the Philippines were eventually overwhelmed by the Japanese and pushed back to Bataan. Many of the Filipinos who stayed continued a guerrilla war. The Japanese occupied Leyte from 1942 to mid-1945.

My father was 19 years old when he ran away from the Japanese occupiers, bartering his way onto a ship going to Luzon by offering to serve as a cook. He caught a ride from Damula-an to Manila, then got on a train that brought him to Cuyapo, Nueva Ecija, a town about 165 km north of Manila along the now-called MacArthur Highway where his older sister, Canora, lived. Cuyapo is a rice-producing area of Luzon, and it was there that my father started a new life as a farmer on a little rented plot of land. It was also where he met my mother, got married, and began a family, which would soon become my eldest sister, Cely, my brother, Glen, my older sister, Liza, myself, and my two younger sisters, Emy and Marie.

What my father lacked in "book learning," he made up for in many other ways. He was a tough man—honest, hardworking, and straightforward to a fault. He would have thought it absurd the way people today obsess over their own personality profiles—whether they're a sanguine or melancholic or how they scored on a DISC test. It seems laughable to me to try to explain to my father the differences in learning and leadership styles and what has come to be known as the "personality ethic." His only concern was a person's work ethic and how well it was established, especially in his two sons.

Underneath the rough exterior, my father was a real people person. In his own way, he was an optimist. He cared about our little town and the people who lived there, especially those he hired from the neighborhood (*barrio*) to work on our farm. And they held him in high regard, because with my father, you always knew where you stood.

Things were not complicated for him. He was very clear about right and wrong. All moral and ethical issues were understood in black and white categories with very few shades of gray. My older brother, Glen, and I used to get lectures on how we should conduct ourselves. "Don't steal, don't lie, work hard, don't quit before you've finished, and never ever disrespect your mother!" His moral code was simple and straightforward, which left very little wiggle room for any who violated it.

When I was about eight years old, I encountered the full force of my father's wrath. I don't particularly remember what I did. All I can recall is I had stolen something and lied about it. In doing so, it was somehow considered disrespectful to my mother as well. With that one act of disobedience, I had transgressed three out of five of my father's uncompromising commandments.

My father could be very loud, especially when he was angry, which was usually because someone had violated his code. He would roar like a lion and shout with a fury that would put the fear of God into young boys' minds. But when the wrong had been made right, it was over.

As expressive as my father was when he was angry, he was equally inhibited when it came to expressing love. That was probably true for many men of his generation. There was not a lot of hugging, kissing, or I-love-yous at home. My father was a tough man who grew up in a tough place at a tough time. He saw giving into emotions as a sign of weakness, a luxury we could not afford. Whenever my brother or I were on the verge of tears, our father would step in.

"Stop it right now! Why are you crying? Boys don't cry!"

I had assumed this was the way things were supposed to be and the way I was supposed to be. The first time either of my parents heard me say "I love you" was after I had become a follower of Christ.

Even though my father was loud and angry, it didn't affect my relationship with him. I knew he loved me even though he never said it. I knew he was proud of me, though he showed his approval in as few words as possible. I was even convinced that I was my father's favorite, though my sisters and brother might disagree.

My father, Buena Ventura Cabiling, was the paradigm of toughness and responsibility, a real man's man. He didn't involve himself in politics or religion but would not hesitate to step up to any challenge he deemed important. Growing up in his house, I constantly measured myself by his standard and always craved his approval. My father's imprint was pressed into my life very deeply. The toughness to endure, the determination to finish what I start, the refusal to quit—much of that came from him.

DOWNHILL TO THE FINISH

My father was a chain smoker who was eventually (though not surprisingly) diagnosed with esophageal cancer in 1989. What was surprising was that he totally stopped smoking and drinking after the diagnosis—a 180-degree reversal that was completely out of character for him. He seemed to have adopted his own mission, giving unsolicited advice to his friends in order to get them to stop drinking and smoking.

The news of my father's sickness ushered in a sense of impending doom, like a dark cloud hanging over our heads. However, there was a genuine blessing in the midst of all the gloom. The changes in my father were like rays of sunlight. Besides abandoning his bad habits, he became more open and approachable—a transformation of his tough demeanor that was almost too shocking to believe. We were all waiting for the explosive father to return.

My father had been baptized a Catholic, but he rarely attended Mass. The sacrament of Confession and my father never seemed to fit together very well. At some point in his life, perhaps in his early years, he had grown cynical about religion and the church. In terms of his faith and the race he had to run, somewhere along the way he had become weary, gotten injured, or lost his way. On one occasion we were sitting by the stairs, and I mustered the courage to preach the gospel to him. To my amazement, he didn't shut me down or ridicule me as he had before. He just sat there with me, listening attentively. He was still listening as I led him in a prayer. Whether or not his attentiveness was simply for my sake, only God knows.

My father endured an entire year of cobalt treatments, which caused him to lose a lot of weight and most of his teeth. I again took advantage of his openness to the gospel, and I asked my friend, Winston Reyes, to pray with me for my father's healing. We laid our hands on a handkerchief and believed for God's mighty power to heal. I gave the handkerchief to my mother and explained about the account in Acts 19:12. I told her to put the handkerchief on my father's neck as an act of faith. I can't be sure what did or did not happen in the following weeks, but my father, who seemed to have been on death's doorstep, lived for another 11 years.

After a decade of being cancer-free, my father's old enemy came back with a vengeance. This time, he was reluctant to be subjected to more cobalt treatments. Under everyone's persistent encouragement, he tried it for several weeks, then stopped. The treatments were very hard on him, maybe because he was older. He refused to take his medicine and became very irritable and difficult to be around. In some ways, you could say that the old Buena Ventura Cabiling had returned. But given the way he was suffering, I choose not to hold him accountable for that last year.

We finally convinced him to see a specialist at the Philippine General Hospital. Several family members had a private conversation with the doctor, who told us frankly: "Your father is in his 70s, and the operation is very risky. My advice is to just let him enjoy the remaining days of his life." We decided to stop pressuring him to have the operation.

His health rapidly declined. It was very painful to see him this way; the once strong and quick-witted man had become so feeble and disoriented. It's painful for any son or daughter to watch a parent mentally or physically fade away. During one of his unannounced trips to Manila, I asked him, "What do you want to do with the time you have left?"

He answered, "I want to go back to Leyte, to die there and be buried next to my parents."

After my mother agreed to let him return to his hometown, my eldest sister, Cely, accompanied him there in July 2000. Our relatives welcomed him and celebrated his return. As Cely and her son, Kim, were leaving, my father shouted, "Cely, thank you for bringing me back home." My other siblings, especially Liza, lent a hand financially to help support his last moments. He died a few months later on November 9, 2000. Upon learning of my father's passing, my mother, my older sister, Liza, my youngest sister, Marie, and I went to Leyte to bury him next to his parents, as he had wished. I conducted the funeral service with the help of a local pastor who spoke Cebuano.

My father has continued to have a great impact on my life. When I was exhausted during some of the *RUN50* stages and in many other races, I could hear him saying, "Come on, Bong (my nickname), stop complaining! Quit feeling sorry for yourself and finish what you started!"

When I was overcome with fear after hearing the news of our newborn son's severe physical handicaps, it was as if I could hear my father shouting, "Stop it, Bong! Boys don't cry! Get in there and support your wife!"

On many other occasions, particularly in the most difficult times, my father's toughness, persistence, and simple code became a source of strength and clarity. Only on two occasions did I actually cry during or after a race. I've come to understand that there's nothing wrong with boys shedding a few tears. I understood my father's voice in my head as, *Don't give into your emotions. Don't let them control you!*

THE VALLEY OF DECISION

On September 21, Day 14 of *RUN50*, the goal was to run from Mahaplag to Dulag. It started, as usual, with a short prayer. My heart was light, and I felt encouraged since I had several pacers from Victory Cebu. As dawn broke through the darkness, I could better see the road, the green grass, and the trees. It was a beautiful place. I understood then why my father had wanted to go back to this province and why he asked to be buried here. Though I wasn't born there, I felt a sense of belonging.

On that day, I had a compelling desire to go off-course and visit my father's gravesite. It had been 15 years since his passing, but I had not returned. This time, I had an opportunity to go back and say thank you. It was my hazard, my temptation to take a detour from my commitment to *RUN50*.

As I approached the fork in the road, I realized how much I missed my father, that his death had left a large hole in my heart. Suddenly, I was overwhelmed with loneliness and sadness. Memories of my father that had been buried deep in my mind came flooding back. As every step brought me nearer to the fork, I knew that I was running toward a decision: turn left to visit his gravesite or continue to Dulag. By the time I reached the fork, it was daylight. I paused for a few moments, looked around, and thought to myself, *So this is where I would need to turn to see my father's gravesite.*

I stayed the course and continued toward Dulag, with my father's voice in my head saying, "Bong, stay on course; finish your race."

RUN50 CHALLENGE

"Another of the disciples said to him, 'Lord, let me first go and bury my father.' And Jesus said to him, 'Follow me, and leave the dead to bury their own dead'" (Matthew 8:21,22). It's worth noting that, unlike the rich young ruler who had balked at Jesus' challenge to sell all his possessions and "come, follow me" (Mark 10:21), this was "another of the disciples." In other words, he was not someone deciding whether or not to follow; he was an existing disciple wanting to take a detour that could certainly be considered a worthy cause—like visiting my father's gravesite. I've heard it said on numerous occasions, "The enemy of the best is the good." It's running a good course but not necessarily the race that God has set before you. I had a compelling reason to run (for my son Philip and the Real LIFE scholars) and an equally compelling reason to run off-course (to honor my father). Both had merit.

That dilemma, and others like it, remind me of the words of the Prophet Samuel. In 1 Samuel 15, King Saul grew weary waiting for Samuel to show up and offer the sacrifice. As the day of the battle drew near, Saul felt compelled to take matters into his own hands and offer the sacrifice. When Samuel arrived and saw what Saul had done, he asked, "Has the Lord as great delight in burnt offerings and sacrifices, as in obeying the voice of the Lord? Behold, to obey is better than sacrifice, and to listen than the fat of rams" (1 Samuel 15:22).

The *RUN50* challenge is this:

What are the hazards that will potentially keep you from finishing your race?

How weary do you have to be before you quit?

Are there unresolved issues in your experience that have injured your faith?

Are you tempted to take a detour to pursue a good thing at the cost of pursuing God's best?

Successful athletes train for mental toughness as well as for physical skills and endurance. Pastor Steve Murrell refers to those habits as "the same old boring strokes." Meditating on God's Word, the confession of faith, time in prayer, and practicing other spiritual disciplines will, over time, help us develop resilient faith and mental toughness to overcome all hazards and finish our race.

03
STARTING LINE
THE BEGINNING OF ANOTHER RACE

Christ, who said to the disciples, "Ye have not chosen me, but I have chosen you," can truly say to every group of Christian friends, "Ye have not chosen one another but I have chosen you for one another."

C.S. LEWIS in *The Four Loves*
Author

For you are my lamp, O Lord, and my God lightens my darkness. For by you I can run against a troop, and by my God I can leap over a wall.

2 SAMUEL 22:29,30

After four years at St. Pius X Institute, a Catholic high school in Cuyapo, I went to Manila to enroll at Adamson University. The Adamson campus was located on San Marcelino Street in Manila. Initially, it was a cultural shock. I had come to the big city as a farm boy from Cuyapo, Nueva Ecija, in Central Luzon. Because of my mother's influence, I was (at best) a nominal Seventh-day Adventist. I had come to Adamson to study engineering in another Catholic university. The biggest adjustments to living in the city were the smog and the masses of humanity crammed into small spaces. Having lived in the province all my life, "normal" for me had always been clean air and open spaces. My body revolted, and I was often sick. I was also lonely. I missed my family, the familiar sounds, and the daily routine of life on the farm. In Cuyapo, I'd walk through the different districts with my friends, making small talk. I had to fight a strong desire to pack my bag and take the next bus back to Nueva Ecija.

It was at Adamson that I discovered running. It might be more accurate to say that I didn't find running; it sort of found me. I had tried basketball (since everyone else seemed to be doing it), without much success. However, in my second year of college, I simply discovered that **I was a runner**. The difference is quite amazing—when what you do is just an extension of who you are and how you see yourself.

Unlike a lot of people, I didn't begin to run because of a New Year's resolution, and I didn't run because someone pressured me into it. I began to run because I **am** a runner. I became an ultramarathoner because I began to see myself as a runner with ultra-clarity.

It got to the point where I was going through running shoes pretty quickly. My older sister, Liza, was a nurse working in Saudi Arabia. Whenever she planned a trip back to the Philippines, she would ask, "Bong, what do you want for *pasalubong*?" The answer was always running shoes. What else does a runner need?

In the city, I eventually got used to the smog. But the loneliness among a sea of unfamiliar faces was harder. Back in Cuyapo, I felt like I knew everyone, they knew me, and they knew my family, which made it harder for me to get away with anything. If I was getting into trouble, my mother and father were sure to hear about it from someone, if not everyone. We all felt responsible for one another. I was used to a sense of being connected and valued. We all had a long history together. That was all I had ever known before arriving in Manila and attending Adamson University.

I joined the Gamma Sigma Pi fraternity in my second year. It might have been my way of trying to get back that feeling of connectedness and belonging, but it was not one of my better life decisions. There was a lot of partying and drinking. Many of my "brothers" turned out to be war freaks—to say that they had unresolved issues would be putting it in the mildest possible terms. They were constantly getting into brawls and gang fights with other fraternities. They seemed to be filled with anger and rage over anything and everything.

Those were turbulent times in the Philippines. In 1983, during my second year at Adamson, the political situation was rapidly escalating into a national crisis. Student protests and riots, which were quickly growing into a popular revolt, were just the kind of thing to channel the angry rage of radical student groups—and many of my fraternity brothers.

Senator Benigno "Ninoy" Aquino was at that time a staunch critic of the president, Ferdinand Marcos. Marcos had held onto dictatorial power with the help of martial law since 1972. However, the president's health was rapidly declining. Fearing that this would cause a violent power struggle between radical factions, Aquino decided to return to the Philippines from a three-year exile in the United States.

On August 21, 1983, Senator Ninoy Aquino was assassinated on the tarmac of the Manila International Airport by a single shot to the head. The assassination shocked and outraged many Filipinos, many of whom had lost confidence in the Marcos administration.

Ferdinand Marcos had grown up in the Ilocos region near Central Luzon, and both of my parents were hard-core supporters. I was named Ferdinand after the president, and my younger sister, Emy, was named Imelda after his wife. My parents remained loyal to Marcos to the end, dismissing the accusations against him as baseless and politically motivated. But the unrest had spread all throughout the Philippines, even to Central Luzon and Cuyapo, Nueva Ecija.

By the end of 1983, the Philippines went into a full-blown economic recession. Investors pulled their money out to put it in more stable markets. Anti-government outrage sparked by Aquino's assassination was sweeping over the general populace. The usually passive business community had even begun to protest because of the flight of capital. But nowhere was the revolt more intense than among students attending universities along C. M. Recto Avenue. These University Belt (U-Belt) campuses were the places where leftist, communist, and anti-Marcos movements had gained a foothold. Almost every day, thousands of activist students with clenched fists and the standard red banners would march down Recto Avenue on their way to the presidential palace. At the barricades along the foot of Mendiola Bridge, the students confronted the army and the riot police. The tension in the confrontations increased each day.

Even with militant groups staging rallies left and right, when I became a Christian, I stood my ground and believed in righteousness in the government. Instead of violently opposing and rebelling against duly elected leaders, our Bible study group was preaching the gospel, making disciples, and actively pursuing leadership positions.

We could do this because an amazing thing happened in June of 1984 amidst the chaos in Manila. Sixty-five American short-term missionaries, most of them university students on their summer break, arrived in Manila and set up nightly evangelistic meetings at the Girl Scouts Auditorium.

The first time I saw any of the Americans was on June 23 on San Marcelino Street, which runs through the Adamson University campus. The street was under construction, and all traffic was being rerouted. Several of the American girls took advantage of the detour and were out in the middle of the street dancing to Christian worship music coming out of a boom box. They all wore long, white dresses like they were going to a formal. I watched because the girls were very pretty, but to me, it seemed so out of place. Pretty girls in long dresses, dancing to Christian music in a construction area, during a season of student riots—it was about as weird and uncool as anything I had ever seen. I actually felt embarrassed for them. So I walked on.

The team of dancing girls was giving out flyers promoting a rock-and-roll seminar the American missionaries were sponsoring. The idea seemed to take the weirdness to another level. American college students coming to Manila as missionaries, playing rock-and-roll music in the Girl Scouts building? I had to check this out.

Back in the early 1980s, rock and roll was as much about clothes as it was music. My room was decorated with a poster of the band KISS. I was a big fan, and those guys wore the most outrageous costumes ever. I had no intention of showing up at a rock concert looking like a civil engineering student. So I went back to my apartment and put on a black vest, 501 jeans, and leather slippers. It sounds crazy now to say it, but dressed and ready for some hard-core rock and roll, I was off to the Girl Scouts Auditorium.

The music playing over the big speaker system when I got there was loud, hard, and actually pretty good, but I didn't recognize the band. It was certainly not my first taste of rock and roll. According to the Seventh-day Adventists, rock and roll was the devil's music, and listening to it was like Edmund from C.S. Lewis's Narnia series eating Turkish Delight—and not being able to stop. Rock and roll would, without a doubt, lead to all manner of moral corruption. I learned later that the music playing was by a band called Petra, known in the 1980s for hard rock with Christian lyrics. Occasionally, I picked up on some of the words and felt a lesser sense of my mother's frowning, though it was laughable to imagine Petra's music playing in our church back in Nueva Ecija. I would have lingered outside a bit longer, checking things out before deciding to go in. However, the pouring rain didn't allow for much hesitation. It was either a go or no-go situation.

The auditorium was filled to overflowing. I went inside and looked around but didn't see any of my classmates or fraternity brothers. Assuming they were in there somewhere, I sat down and listened to the music playing in the background. Eventually, one of the Americans got up and began the seminar, *Rock 'n' Roll: A Search for God*. Halfway through the presentation, I was beginning to think the Seventh-day Adventists might have been right all along. Seeing the subliminal artwork on album covers was a bit spooky. Listening to AC/DC's *Highway to Hell* played backwards sounded like a demonic voice saying over and over, "Start to smoke marijuana; start to smoke marijuana." The presentation, with all the demonic images, lyrics, and statements from popular rock stars, was really beginning to freak me out. I realized soon after that the American missionaries weren't there on a crusade against rock music.

The reason they had come to Manila became apparent when one of the missionaries about my age went on stage and began to speak.

That man was Rice Broocks, a quick-witted, story-telling, big-and-tall Texan who could grab an audience and hold them on the edge of their seats. Growing up, my biggest religious influences had been my mother and grandmother. Our chapel services were mostly attended by women. My father and older brother had never bothered with religion, so to me, religion was a woman's thing. In an extreme contrast, Rice Broocks's style was dynamic, engaging, forceful, manly, youthful, and relevant. Most of all, there was no hint of the religiosity to which I was so accustomed. If the objective of the rock-and-roll seminar and Rice Broocks was to get my attention—well, it was surely working.

His description of my life and my lukewarm spiritual condition was frighteningly accurate. I felt like I was standing in front of a torrent of truth as he preached the gospel of Jesus Christ with unreserved passion and conviction. I can't say that I'd never heard the gospel before. I heard it every Sunday in church with my mother and sisters. But that night, it was like I was hearing it for the very first time. The guys sitting next to me were actually crying as Rice asked the question, "If you died tonight, where would you spend eternity?"

Rice continued to press the issue by challenging anyone who was unsure about their eternal standing with God to come down front and pray to receive Jesus Christ as Lord and Savior. Many of the people in the auditorium began to stream forward. I felt goose bumps, my heart pounding, and the power of something trying to pry me out of that seat. Of course, I now know it was the convicting power of the Holy Spirit shining His spotlight into the deep, dark corners of my soul. I kept telling myself, *I'm not going down there. No, not tonight. Too many people here know me.* And so I sat there, tightly clutching the edge of my seat.

People continued to make their way to the front. *If I can just hold on a little longer,* I thought to myself, *perhaps I can escape.* That seems so silly to me now. Why would I want to escape the grace of God, His forgiveness, or the presence of His Holy Spirit? The primary reason seems to be that we don't want to humble ourselves and admit our need. But no matter how I tried to assure myself that I was okay with God—that even with my shortcomings, I was better than most—that night, the Holy Spirit was unrelenting. I even tried to strike some kind of bargain with God, promising to get back to Him later. Maybe I would have received Christ and surrendered to Him at another time and place. Sometimes, I wonder what my life would have been like if I had resisted the Holy Spirit that night to the point of walking away.

In the midst of my agony and indecision, someone patted me on the elbow. I never looked around to see if it was an usher or an angel. I simply stood up and ran, not for the door but toward the front.

Just because I ran forward didn't necessarily mean I was ready and willing to surrender unconditionally. I didn't notice any friends or classmates going forward. I was looking straight ahead, not wanting to see or be seen by anyone I knew.

Sitting there by myself clutching my seat had actually caused me to stick out more. No one was paying any attention to me, but I was held back by all my insecurities. I was unwilling to take a stand by going forward, and after most had gone to the front, I was unwilling to take a stand by **not** going forward. Without the moral courage to do one thing or the other, I just followed the crowd.

Looking back on it now, I was just like Peter on the night of the Lord's betrayal. After His arrest, Peter followed the soldiers and the crowd as they took Jesus to stand trial before the council of Jewish leaders (Matthew 26:57,58). Peter followed along and even snuck into the courtyard of Caiaphas, the high priest, but he didn't follow so closely that he would be recognized. And when on three occasions people said to him, "You too are one of His disciples," Peter cursed and angrily denied it. Then, as Jesus had foretold, the rooster crowed (Matthew 26:75).

I was on the doorstep of a new life and radical transformation by the power of the Holy Spirit. The demonic powers of hell must have been screaming. Not wanting to stand out as one of those who had come forward to become a disciple, I slithered my way to the middle, near the center where I was hidden among the crowd. Just then, one of the Americans walked up onto the stage and began taking pictures. Like Peter, the last thing I wanted was to be recognized. *Why,* I thought, *is this guy taking pictures?* Little did I know that the photograph of me with an angry look on my face would later be published in the book *Change the Campus, Change the World* by Rice Broocks.

There were a lot of things I didn't understand about genuine Christianity—about being born again, justification by faith, or following Jesus. All I knew was that I was a sinner who needed a Savior. After asking people to come forward, Rice led us in a prayer for salvation.

I was overwhelmed. Something incredible was happening; I felt God's presence and sensed His forgiveness. One of the Americans, Tim, was standing next to me. After Rice led us all in a prayer, Tim said to me, "Congratulations! I have a verse I'd like to read, if you don't mind." He read Acts 2:38,39, which says, "Repent and be baptized every one of you in the name of Jesus Christ for the forgiveness of your sins, and you will receive the gift of the Holy Spirit. For the promise is for you and for your children and for all who are far off, everyone whom the Lord our God calls to himself."

He then asked, "You've come here to the front and repented of your sins, am I correct?"

"Yes."

"And you're trusting in Christ's sacrifice for your salvation, you're repenting of your sin, and you're giving your life to follow Him. Is that correct?"

"Yes, yes," I said.

"Okay, it says here, 'Repent and be baptized.' Are you willing to get baptized tonight?"

I remember asking, "Uh . . . what religion is this?"

What I was trying to ask (with my less-than-sophisticated theological understanding) was, "Which denomination is this?"

Besides being convicted by the Holy Spirit, the question about where I would spend eternity had struck fear into my heart because I hadn't been baptized. Seven years in Catholic schools had left me with a lot of superstitions about the rite of baptism. Catholics baptize infants; the Seventh-day Adventists do not. I think I'd been waiting for my mother to bring up the subject of baptism. I suppose she was waiting for the Holy Spirit to do His work in me.

Avoiding the denominational question, Tim simply explained that they believe the Bible is the Word of God. Since my mother had been drilling that into me for most of my life, that was good enough for me.

"Yes," I replied boldly. "I want to get baptized!"

We took a jeepney over to the Admiral Hotel on Roxas Boulevard where the Americans were staying. Since I hadn't come to the rock-and-roll seminar that night expecting to get baptized, I didn't have a change of clothes.

"No problem," Tim said. "We'll lend you some shorts."

Seventeen of us paraded through the lobby to the pool out back. I was thin enough to all but disappear when I turned sideways, and the American shorts were way too large. So I went down into the pool and got baptized, holding on for dear life to my shorts, lest I lose them in the waters of baptism. Coming out of the water, they laid hands on me and prayed for me to be filled with the Holy Spirit. I was so cold, I don't recall if I was speaking in tongues or if my teeth were just chattering. All I knew was that something supernatural was happening to me.

We changed back into our clothes, and Al Manamtam, a Filipino on the American team, went over everything again—faith in Christ's sacrifice, repentance, water baptism, and baptism in the Holy Spirit.

THE FIRST SUNDAY

The Americans used the Girl Scouts Auditorium on Taft Avenue for all the meetings in the first few weeks, but on Sunday mornings, the worship services were held at the Admiral Hotel. I had given my life to Christ on a Saturday night, jumping in completely with no holds barred. I was totally surrendered (or as surrendered as I knew how to be at that time). I'd learn a lot more about this "surrender" thing as time went on.

"Come back here tomorrow morning," Tim said. "You got a Bible? Great, bring it. See you tomorrow."

I remember walking back to the apartment that I shared with my older sister, Liza, filled with an overflowing happiness. It was what the Apostle Peter referred to as "joy inexpressible and filled with glory" (1 Peter 1:8). I knocked on the door, and Liza let me in. It was 1:00 a.m.

"Where have you been?" she asked. Seeing the joy and glory in my face, she continued, "And what has happened to you?"

I told my astonished sister that I had attended a seminar. That night, alone in my room, I got on my knees and thanked God for everything He had done for me.

Over the years, The Gideons International had distributed Bibles all over the Philippines. I returned to the Admiral Hotel on

Sunday morning with my blue, pocket-sized Gideon New Testament in hand. Arriving early at the hotel, I wasn't sure where to go. Two girls on the team of Americans saw me with my little Bible and asked me in a Southern drawl, "Are you here for the church?"

"Uh, excuse me, say that again?"

"Are you here for the church?"

I was embarrassed because I still couldn't understand them.

"Could you speak a little slower?"

"Are . . . you . . . here . . . for . . . the . . . church?"

I didn't understand. I wasn't going to the church. I had come to the hotel to meet Tim.

Remembering Tim's instruction to bring a Bible, I finally connected the dots. I was at the hotel for a church service.

"Yes, yes. I'm here for the church."

They showed me to the meeting room, where I saw Tim.

"Hey, Ferdie!"

"Hey, Tim, good to see you!"

"We've got a few minutes before it starts. I want to show you something."

Tim gave me a copy of a little tract published by Christian Equippers International entitled *Are You Going to Heaven? Two Question Test Reveals Answer.* After reading through the tract with Tim, we went down to the meeting. That was my first exposure to people who were passionately worshiping God and raising their hands. I had never seen anything like it.

I returned to the Admiral Hotel the next week for the foundations class. Rice Broocks introduced the teacher. I felt that I'd seen this American somewhere before. *Oh yeah,* I thought to myself. *That's the guy who came up on stage and began taking pictures during the altar call—the one who captured the image of me with the angry face.* That was my first introduction to Steve Murrell. I had been angry because I had not wanted to be recognized as one of Christ's followers. However, I was now one of His disciples—baptized, filled with the Holy Spirit, and looking for opportunities to boldly preach the good news.

TWO BANDS OF BROTHERS

I immediately preached the gospel to Tonypet, the fraternity brother who had recruited me for Gamma Sigma Pi, and led him in a prayer of salvation. The rest of my fraternity brothers did not share Tonypet's interest in my newfound faith. My relationship with Jesus Christ and sudden allegiance to Christianity was viewed as disloyalty to the fraternity. Consequently, preaching the gospel to the rest of my frat brothers was met with considerable hostility. Tonypet, my brand new brother in Christ, stood in the gap as a mediator between me and the tribe of angry protestors and warriors. He did his best to explain my new life and allegiance to them, but since I had rejected all the drinking and partying, they took it as a sign of rejection of them. I tried to show them God's love and acceptance, but in the end, they gave me up to my newfound faith, and I faded away from their memory.

It seemed that God had chosen to place me in another band of brothers. In his book *The Four Loves*, C.S. Lewis wrote about his little circle of friends that included Hugo Dyson, Charles Williams, and J.R.R. Tolkien: "Christ, who said to the disciples, 'Ye have not chosen me, but I have chosen you,' can truly say to every group of Christian friends, 'Ye have not chosen one another but I have chosen you for one another.'"

Sometimes, I think about how Jesus chose the twelve. What kind of selection process would you conduct for such an elite squad of disciples, commissioned with the sole responsibility of "going into all the world" to change it? On the surface, the selection seemed to be quite casual, even random. Andrew, a disciple of John the Baptist, ran into Jesus and began to follow Him. Andrew immediately went and got his brother, Peter. Then Peter introduced his business partners, James and John, to Jesus. Philip was from Bethsaida, the hometown of Peter and Andrew. After hearing Jesus, Philip went and brought his neighbor, Nathanael.

This is how the gospel works its way into and through friendships. Those who encounter Christ immediately invite friends, relatives, and classmates to "come and see." It was the two friends, J.R.R. Tolkien and Hugo Dyson, who introduced C.S. Lewis, a former atheist, to Christ.

Steve began discipling me in the second week of the outreach in the Philippines. A few years later, I began discipling a student named Rico, whose mother, Cely, was already in church. Rico brought his sister, Noreena, to church, then his younger brother, Roy, then Jay, then Jolina. Eventually, his father, Johnny, started attending a Victory group with businessmen, and responded to the gospel. Rico's sister, Ria, soon followed. Around the same time, Rico's classmate, Vinay, came around. Then he brought his sister, Varsha, to church, who came with their mother, Sushma. And so on. And that's primarily how Victory has grown for over three decades—new believers inviting their family and friends to join them in a Victory group for small group discipleship, going through *ONE 2 ONE* with them, and helping them follow Jesus.

In retrospect, I've come to realize that there is nothing random about the power of the Holy Spirit working in groups of friends. God sovereignly puts people together for His purpose.

RUN50 CHALLENGE

I've never been more convinced of God's sovereign calling to those of us who were there at the beginning, as well as to those who are being added to lead the next generations of disciples. None of us just aimlessly wander into the kingdom of God. We have been aimed by God's calling and choosing.

The same thing continues to this day. New believers create lists of their friends with the intent of inviting them to a Victory group. If five of those individuals are transformed by God's gift of salvation, the gospel makes inroads into five more friendship groups. That's how Victory has grown from 160 students at the end of the first month to what it is today. Don't ever think of yourself as merely one of the many Victory group leaders. There's nothing "mere" about that. Victory group leaders and new believers engaging their not-yet-believing friends is the essential engine of spreading the gospel.

The *RUN50* challenge is this: Whether you're a new Victory group leader or someone who's been leading for a few years, do you have a list of family members and friends you are actively engaging with the gospel?

04
BASIC TRAINING
GROWING AS YOU'RE GOING

Tell me and I forget, teach me and I may remember, involve me and I learn.

BENJAMIN FRANKLIN
United States Inventor and Founding Father

. . . and what you have heard from me in the presence of many witnesses entrust to faithful men, who will be able to teach others also.

2 TIMOTHY 2:2

After two weeks at the Girl Scouts Auditorium, the American team leased the Tandem Cinema basement as our regular gathering place. The space underneath the run-down movie theater was where they ran the leaky sewer pipes. Like all the other buildings around the area, the basement was a nasty, stinky, subterranean cavern with no windows and no air-conditioning—a place unfit for humans, but perfect for rats and other pests. It would, however, seat several hundred people, and it was located in U-Belt, right in the middle of the largest concentration of colleges and universities in the Philippines. It was also the epicenter of the anti-Marcos student revolts. If you wanted to start a church to change a nation, it was the perfect place! The auditorium took an enormous amount of work to clean up. We all hauled trash, scrubbed the walls, and polished the pavement for a solid week to make the underground facility habitable.

The Americans had arrived in June and would leave in a month, three weeks from the day I received Christ as my Lord and Savior. The team of 65 Americans (mostly students) was moving on to an evangelistic campaign in Seoul, South Korea, similar to the one launched in Manila. They frequently reminded us of the short time they had with us and put us through constant training. As the day of their departure drew near, the reality began to sink in—who was going to preach? Who was going to follow up new believers? Who was going to teach the foundations class? There were many other leadership issues we didn't even know to worry about. None of us had had any more than a few weeks' experience as Christians, let alone with Christian ministry.

Steve Murrell was responsible for ministering to the students who had responded to Rice Broocks's message. He helped new believers like me understand grace, faith, and repentance. He also taught us about the Holy Spirit and prepared us for water baptism. And so, with the team's departure at hand, he began training us to do the same thing with the next wave of Filipinos who would come to Christ.

Steve was put in charge of our crash course in Christianity and our basic training for ministry. I remember the day we were designated to help the new believers who had been responding to the gospel message.

"But I've only been saved a week!" I said.

Steve immediately replied, "Yes, but this guy has only been saved three minutes, and to him you're a spiritual giant. Remember I told you to read the Gospel of Mark? How far have you read?"

"I'm done with Mark," I said, "and I'm almost finished with Luke."

Then Steve stated what became the slogan for those early days: "As long as you stay one chapter ahead, you can disciple that new believer. But if he passes you, then he'll disciple you."

LEARNING BY DOING

Discipleship training for us was both biblical (foundations classes) and practical ("follow me and do what I do"). I remember a time as a young believer several months old in the Lord. Steve was on stage during the worship service signaling me to come up. I was an usher and thought he was asking for something to drink. So I poured a glass of water, went up on stage, and tried to hand it to him. But he whispered to me to stay there with him. I then realized that he wanted me to observe him as he ministered to those who had come forward.

Another time, right after the worship service, he was with a few guys seated in a corner near the stage. Again, I saw him giving me a signal to come and join him. So I pulled up a chair and sat there listening to the conversation. One of them must have made the connection between forgiveness and the sacrament of Confession, because he was going through a long list of his misdeeds. After Steve explained the gospel to him, they got down on their knees to pray to receive Christ as Lord and Savior. It looked odd that they were both on their knees while I was just sitting there. So I decided to get down on my knees, too. I was thinking, *What am I doing? Why am I on my knees? Does he want me to pray to receive Christ again?* Then it hit me, *Ah yes, I am assisting Steve. This is part of my training!*

Then, at one particular midweek service, Steve had some of the young disciples preach. Four of us—Jun Escosar, Elsa Acebo, Gigi Lim (now Gigi Escosar), and myself—were instructed to preach for five minutes each. We had pretty much exhausted our biblical knowledge within those five minutes, but we were full of faith and on fire with the Holy Spirit in our lives. Jun went first, and I, being the last, was asked to call for people to give their lives to Christ. I made a passionate appeal, expecting people to sprint forward as I had done a few weeks before. Perhaps our little four-part sermon had left them totally confused because nobody responded, or seemed moved or convicted—or so I thought.

Right after the service, a girl came running toward me crying and saying, "I want to give my life to Christ!" Suddenly, I went from being totally discouraged at our first attempt at preaching to being filled with extraordinary joy. That might have been the moment the gift of evangelism was awakened in me. Sometimes, the gifts of the Holy Spirit are only realized when we step out in faith to exercise them. From that day on, I've relentlessly appealed to people to surrender their lives to Christ. In the days that followed, at the conclusion of each message, Steve would hand me the microphone so that I could invite people to come to Christ.

Steve taught me how to evangelize—not just through classes, but in the campuses. On one particular day at the University of Santo Tomas (UST), he asked me to present the gospel to a medical student. I considered it a smooth-sailing and effective gospel presentation. However, when the student disagreed with me and said he did not want to put his trust in Christ, I simply and boldly pronounced his sentence: "Then you'll go to hell!"

As was his custom, Steve gave me an evaluation on our way back to the Tandem Cinema basement. He asked me why I said what I had said. I tried to defend my motives, but Steve reminded me of my actual words. He showed me that although I might have been sincere in my presentation, it had come out very differently. It was as if I had said, "If you don't want to accept Christ, you can just go to hell!"

I felt horrible about what I had said and how I had dishonored the Lord and the gospel. I also felt sorry for the guy, who I never saw again.

Back at the Tandem Cinema basement, we joined the other young believers who had also been to the campuses. Still feeling ashamed of my on-campus performance, I took a seat at the very back. Each group was sharing wonderful testimonies of students' responses to their gospel presentation. When Steve stood up to share our experience, I braced myself for the story of how I had cursed the poor guy and told him to go to hell. It would probably serve as a lesson for everyone on what not to do. Instead, Steve's report went something like this: "Ferdie is the best evangelist I have ever been with on campus!"

My eyes began to sweat. (Remember, real men don't cry.)

LEADING WITH THE IDEA OF LEAVING

Steve has always referred to himself as someone with very little evangelistic giftings. I often wondered in the beginning if it was just an act of self-effacement, his goal all along being to encourage and empower us to preach the gospel. Later on, in *WikiChurch*, Steve Murrell (2011, 145) wrote about what his wife, Deborah, said:

"Deborah's response struck right at the heart of the matter. 'From the very beginning,' she said, 'it was never about creating a position or a ministry for ourselves. We were always leading with the idea of leaving.'"

They were preparing eighteen- to twenty-year-old Filipinos to do the ministry and lead the church.

After a month, most of the American team moved on to South Korea. Steve said goodbye to them and remained in Manila to lead the fledgling church. "Pastor Steve," as he came to be known, wound up staying for over 25 years as the founder and senior pastor of Victory. He now serves as the president of Every Nation, a worldwide family of churches and ministries.

It occurred to me a few years later that this must have been what it was like in the early church as the Apostle Paul preached the gospel to the Gentiles in Crete. He won converts and gave them all the training he could before being run out of town but left Titus, one of his young leaders, to do the follow-up. Rice Broocks had recruited Steve, his college roommate, to serve as his right-hand man on the mission trip to the Philippines. As it turned out, Pastor Steve was like Titus. After the church had been planted with the first converts, Titus was left behind in Crete. Like Titus, Pastor Steve "put what remained into order," and appointed "elders in every town" (Titus 1:5). This is how I came to join him in ministry.

TITHE ME TO THE LORD

Toughness and determination came from my father and brother. Empowerment through education came from the women in my family.

My maternal grandfather, Delfin Lozano, had served as a member of the Philippine Scouts. He insisted that his three children devote themselves to their studies. My mother, Paz, and her youngest sister, Lydia, both became teachers. Auntie Lydia was the one who named me by putting "Ferdinand" into the hat. Their brother, Lope, entered the U.S. Naval Academy in 1955 and after graduating, joined the

U.S. Navy. It was Uncle Lope and Auntie Lydia who helped send the six of us to school.

Those two generations, my grandfather and his children, were committed to the future of those who followed and were determined to do whatever it took to give us a good education. It often takes two or three generations for a family to climb out of poverty, but it almost never happens unless someone steps forward to champion their cause. I'm so thankful for the encouragement and sacrifice of my mother's family. Two of my sisters became nurses, and another works in retail. My brother, Glen, finished school and became a seaman. The difference my grandfather and his children made in our lives is why I run for the Real LIFE scholars.

As my time at Adamson University came to a close, I decided to enter full-time ministry. That was (at least in my mind) going to be a big issue. How was I going to explain this to my mother, who had sacrificed so much to put me through college? The time to think it through was running out. Graduation was only a few days away, and I would soon have to go home and explain myself.

Every Sunday throughout my five years in college, my parents would send us rice and vegetables from the farm, along with an envelope containing our allowance from Auntie Lydia. One of our relatives was a bus driver who would bring the package from the province. After every Sunday morning service, it was my duty to go to the bus station to collect the *bayong* (native basket) and the envelope.

On the first Sunday after my graduation, I got the weekly package, then sat down and wrote a letter to my mother.

"*Inang*, thank you for sending me to college all these years. I know this has been a real hardship for you. Please tell my father how much I appreciate you both. From this day on, please don't give me my allowance anymore. Thank you for all the effort and sacrifice."

That didn't exactly announce my decision to become a preacher, but I was building up to that. No doubt my parents had a different plan all worked out in their minds. They, along with Uncle Lope and Auntie Lydia, had ensured I would make it. After graduation, I was expected to go abroad, get a job as a civil engineer, and lend a hand financially so my two younger sisters could join me. My mother and father probably assumed I was out looking for a civil engineering job, but I never really considered it.

I knew my father would not understand why I would turn my back on such opportunities or on the implied responsibility to help my sisters. So I did what most children do in difficult situations like this—I decided to talk to my mother first. As a devout Christian, she represented my best chance at my parents' understanding God's calling and destiny for my life.

It was clear to me that I was called by God to preach the gospel. I just didn't know how to make that clear to my family. I've discovered over the years that rarely is God's calling announced so clearly and loudly that all the skeptics around you can hear it as well. After my graduation, the ministry team, consisting of Jun Escosar, Gigi Lim, Tom Bouvier, and Pastor Steve, gave me a business card since I was supposed to be on staff already as one of Victory's first campus missionaries. However, the person in charge of the finances didn't know it. So, I got my start as an official full-time campus missionary with a calling from God and a business card, but with no salary, no packages from home, and nothing to eat.

My older sister, Liza, was still in college. Instead of me helping her financially, she shared her food from home with me. Every time I went back to our apartment, she would ask me if I had eaten. I would say no, and she would give me something to eat and divide her allowance between the two of us. She knew about my decision to be a pastor rather than a civil engineer, but she neither ridiculed nor criticized me for it.

I knew that I would eventually have to go home and explain my decision. It's one thing to be bold like a lion preaching the gospel on campus. But going home and talking to your parents? Well, that's a different thing altogether. When I could avoid it no longer, I went back to Cuyapo and sat down with my mother. To break the ice, I gave her one of my business cards.

"*Inang*, look at this," I said.

Carefully eyeing the card, she replied, "Yes, I see. But what is this?"

"*Inang*," I said, "I'm going to be in the ministry. I feel like God has called me to be a preacher."

After pausing for a few moments (which felt like hours) as she stared at the card, she looked up at me and asked, "Bong, are you sure?"

"Yes, I am positive. This is God's plan for my life."

After a few more awkward moments I continued, "*Inang*, do you remember when I was little and we would go to the chapel?"

"Yes, I remember."

"You would give us money so we'd have something to give as our tithe?"

"Yes, I remember," she said enthusiastically. Seventh-day Adventists value tithing.

"Look, *Inang*, there are six of us in the family. Would you please just tithe me to the Lord?"

With that, it was settled. Everything seemed to become as clear to her as it had been to me. In the end it all worked out, as my naval-academy uncle continued, with my parents and aunt, to help my sisters finish their studies.

A RUNNING START

In the following years, I began serving as a traveling evangelist in the campuses of Metro Manila. I preached the gospel on many of the U-Belt campuses (University of Santo Tomas, Far Eastern University, University of the East, Centro Escolar University, and Philippine School of Business Administration), in the campuses in the Intramuros area (Lyceum of the Philippines University, Mapúa Institute of Technology, Pamantasan ng Lungsod ng Maynila, and Colegio de San Juan de Letran), in the campuses in the Taft area (Adamson University, Technological University of the Philippines, Philippine Normal College, Philippine Christian University), and later, in De La Salle University, the University of the Philippines in Manila and Diliman, and the Ateneo de Manila University.

Many of those who were reached in the early days became full-time ministers like me. As the work in these campuses grew, we began to develop strong leadership teams. I even started going to the provinces in response to the requests of the pastors there to come and help. I also joined Jun Escosar as he pioneered church-planting endeavors in the provinces. First, we went to Dagupan City, then to Tuguegarao City, where Jonathan Bocobo stayed behind to pastor the new church. Next, we went to Baguio City, where we helped Jojo Henson plant a church. In this Baguio outreach, the gospel transformed the lives of many who eventually became pastors, including Julius Calaycay (Victory Baguio) and Julius Vaquilar (Victory Santiago).

RUN50 CHALLENGE

Are you waiting on God for something? Are you putting aside procrastination, fear, and doubt, and stepping out in faith? Patience is a virtue, but procrastination is not; fear is not; doubt is not. There are many who are waiting oh-so-patiently for a word from God that He's already spoken, for a gift of the Spirit that He's already given, or for a level of maturity that one would never attain without stepping out in faith. Maybe you're like me, with my chance to preach a little five-minute sermon. I grabbed the opportunity and gave it everything I had. In the process of preparing for and delivering that little message, God's calling was confirmed in my heart, and I've been running with that calling and gifting ever since.

05
CHAMPION-SHIP
THE PRACTICE OF STANDING IN THE GAP

I remember as a little boy I ate one meal a day and sometimes slept in the street. I will never forget that, and it inspires me to fight hard, stay strong, and remember all the people of my country (who are) trying to achieve better for themselves.

MANNY PACQUIAO
Senator and Boxer

But as God has not made anything useless in this world, as all beings fulfill obligations or fill a role in this sublime drama of creation, I cannot exempt myself from this duty, and small though it be, I too have a mission to fulfill, as for example: alleviating the sufferings of my fellowmen.

DR. JOSE RIZAL
Philippine National Hero

It will become a sign and a witness to the Lord of hosts in the land of Egypt; for they will cry to the Lord because of oppressors, and He will send them a Savior and a Champion, and He will deliver them.

ISAIAH 19:20 (NASB)

After the 1984 outreach, my remaining years in college were spent preaching the gospel and serving in the church. By 1986, I was living in what we called the Victory staff house. At that time, I was still running alone. During the revolution that deposed President Ferdinand Marcos, most of Metro Manila was shut down. One day, after my housemates (Jonathan Bocobo, Joseph Carodan, Richard Gambe, John Go, Rocky Hashmi, Gene Manaois, Jess Salas, and Arnie Suson) and I prayed in the living room, we ran from the staff house on Mendoza Guazon Street in Paco to Luneta Park and back—a round trip of 11 km. After that one-time "revolutionary run," I went back to my solo running—that is, when I could carve out some free time from preaching and making disciples.

It was in 2006 that I finally found my running buddies. Junn Besana, Nixon Ng, Juray Mora, Ado Bernardo, and I agreed to run every Saturday morning around Bonifacio Global City (BGC), sometimes along Roxas Boulevard, each time covering about 10 to 15 km. Times and distances changed depending on our weekend schedules, but we always made it a point to end the run with a hearty breakfast at Banapple. In those early days, we referred to our little group of runners as the "Running Freaks." It was only after I had run the *102-km Bataan Death March* in 2011 that I branded myself the "Running Pastor."

Up until that race, my friends and I would simply run until we were out of time or energy, measuring ourselves against one another by who was the most spent when we decided to quit. Frank Shorter, a men's marathon gold medalist in the *1972 Munich Olympics*, once said, "I want my time spent running to serve as [its own] reward." That's what we had been doing—running for the pleasure of it.

We had read about organized races and dreamed of someday being part of a race with lots of runners, a starting gun, bib numbers, and everything else. Having never been in an official race, we didn't know what to expect or what we were missing. In 2008, Nike hosted the *Nike+ Human Race*, a 10-km run from McKinley to Bayani Road and back. Our running group immediately signed up. I had recently passed my 42nd birthday, and so my daughter, Elizabeth (Elle), came out to see her old father compete.

The *Nike+ Race* was a new experience for us. We were in a real race, competing against one another, a clock, and our previous best efforts. The Apostle Paul's exhortation to the Corinthian church about the race they were running highlighted the difference between running for recreation and running with a purpose. "Do you not know that in a race all the runners run, but only one receives the prize? So run that you may obtain it. . . . I do not run aimlessly" (1 Corinthians 9:24,26). Crossing the finish line gave us all a big shot of triumphant adrenalin. We had been a tiny group of running freaks. The *Nike+ Human Race* turned us into running addicts.

THE FIRST MARATHON

My first full marathon was the *Philippine International Marathon 2009: Run for Pasig River*, a course that crossed ten bridges around Metro Manila. The purpose of the run was to raise awareness of the Pasig River project, as well as funds for the cleanup. It was a solo run for me, without my usual running buddies, but it was an eye-opening experience—doing what I loved to do, and at the same time raising money for a good cause. The *Run for Pasig River* had several categories—3 km, 5 km, 10 km, and 42 km. In the U.S. and in other places around the world, the term "marathon" refers to a run of precisely 42 km (26.2 mi). According to the Greek legend, in 490 BC, Pheidippides ran 42 km from the battlefield near the town of Marathon to Athens in order to announce the defeat of the invading Persians. Upon reaching the Athenian agora, Pheidippides shouted "Nike!" (meaning "victory"). He then collapsed from exhaustion and died. In the Philippines, the word "marathon" is applied in a more generic fashion, used simply as a reference to a long run. Therefore, anything over 5 km might be considered "marathon-ish."

After the 42-km *Run for Pasig River*, we joined several 21-km races, one of those being *Run BGC* in 2010. I was the only one of our running group who joined, but my involvement turned out to be providential. At the finish line, I met another runner, Joshua Suarez. He recognized me and introduced himself as a member of Victory Fort.

Joshua asked, "You have run a marathon, right?"

"Yes," I said.

"Would you consider joining me in a 100-km run?"

"A hundred km! Are you kidding? How can there be such a race?"

"Well, there is," he replied. "It's happening next year, and I've been preparing for it."

As Joshua began to share his own running experiences, faith began to rise up in me. Before the conversation was over, I had caught the vision. Though the distance was over twice as far as I had ever run before, like the seeds in the English fairy tale *Jack and the Beanstalk*, the idea began to grow quickly in my mind. I said to myself, *I can do that!*

"How long and how hard would I have to train for such a challenge?"

"You have time to catch up," Joshua said. "You can train with me." He persisted, "Will you run the 102 km with me?"

"Sure, why not?" I said.

We shook hands, made some training plans, and were about to part ways when I asked, "By the way, what's the name of the race?"

He replied, "The *Bataan Death March*."

THE 1942 BATAAN DEATH MARCH

After the fall of Manila in 1942, the Japanese forced the retreat of over 80,000 Filipino and American soldiers onto the Bataan Peninsula. The Filipino and American forces struggled to hold out against overwhelming odds until reinforcements arrived; however, the U.S. Pacific Fleet was so crippled at Pearl Harbor that no help was on the way. The combined forces resisted for three months but were forced to surrender on April 9, 1942. After the fall of Bataan, the surviving 64,000 Filipinos and 12,000 Americans were rounded up by the Japanese and forced to march 102 km from Mariveles at the southern end of the Bataan Peninsula to San Fernando, Pampanga. From there, prisoners were transported by rail another 14 km to Capas, Tarlac. Then followed another forced march to the former Philippine Army camp known as Camp O'Donnell—a total distance of 155 km from Mariveles. Thousands died from hunger, exhaustion, and exposure. Many more were executed by the Japanese. According to the *Encyclopaedia Britannica* (2017), of the 76,000 Filipinos and Americans who began the Bataan Death March in Mariveles, only 54,000 survived Camp O'Donnell.

The 2011 race traced the route of the original Bataan Death March in 1942, beginning on March 5 (a month before the April 9 march started in 1942) at the 00-km historical marker, and ending at the railway station in San Fernando where the Filipino and American prisoners had been loaded into boxcars. Just as the first modern Olympic marathon on April 10, 1896 was a reenactment of the 42-km route from Marathon to Athens, the *2011 Bataan Death March* retraced the historic route from Mariveles to San Fernando.

To prepare for the 102-km run, Joshua suggested that I join the *Tagaytay-Nasugbu 50K Run* in November 2010, which was organized by retired General Jovie Narcise of the Philippine Association of Ultrarunners. It was actually more than a suggestion. Finishing the 50-km race under the time limit was a prerequisite for joining the *102-km Bataan Death March*. I was the only one of our running group who had initially signed up for the 50-km in November 2010. However, it wasn't long before Junn Besana joined me; then Alden Meneses, and then Paul Pajo. In the end, five of us from Victory entered the race.

We mutually agreed that we were not satisfied with just running without a purpose; we wanted to run for something—or someone. We wanted to monetize our hobby to help those in need. After our first official competitive race, my first marathon, and our first ultramarathon, the five of us were itching to "run with an aim"—to run for something or someone in the upcoming *Bataan Death March* ultramarathon. And there was no doubt among us what that cause would be. We would run for the Real LIFE Foundation scholars.

REAL LIFE FOUNDATION SCHOLARS

Real LIFE Foundation exists to honor God by serving the poor in the Philippines through educational assistance, character development, and community service. By raising funds for Real LIFE, we would be instrumental in giving financial aid to its high school and college scholars. Here's one example.

In March 2013, my daughter Elle and I attended the graduation ceremony of Real LIFE Foundation. We were invited to the event to see one of the scholars, Van Estrano, walk across the stage as a graduate of the University of the Philippines Diliman with a Bachelor of Arts in Linguistics. Van was our family's "Adopted Scholar," and I'm very proud of her.

In 2008, Van and one of her siblings were in college. Two others were in high school, and two more were in elementary. Their father's meager salary could not support the education of all his six children, though they were enrolled in public schools. Van happened to visit her teachers in San Francisco High School, Mrs. Ester Libunao and Mrs. Beliarmina Dar Juan, both after-class Victory group leaders. Talking with Van about her schooling, they discovered that she constantly struggled to come up with the money for tuition fees, school supplies, and food. On the spot, they interviewed her for a Real LIFE scholarship. She was connected to Victory and introduced to people who helped her understand Christ's finished work on the cross. Van went through *ONE 2 ONE* and finished her *Victory Weekend* the following month—that was the start of her discipleship journey. As a result, she preached the gospel to her three sisters and brought them to church. She's still believing for the salvation of her parents and other siblings.

As we watched Van being honored as a Real LIFE scholar, I couldn't help but think of the sacrifices my family had made for my education, and how privileged we were to have done the same for Van. Currently, she is working at the Commission on Higher Education. She handles the Scholarship for Graduate Studies (SGS) grants of the CHED K to 12 Transition Program. On top of that, Van is a Victory group leader and serves as a vocalist in the music ministry of Victory Katipunan.

I was able to finish the *102-km Bataan Death March* in 2011 in a run time of 17 hours, 17 minutes, and 39 seconds (17:17:39). However, more important than my new personal record, each of the runners from Victory secured pledges from donors of PHP 1,000 per kilometer (PHP 102,000 per runner). Together, we were able to raise over half a million pesos for Real LIFE scholars like Van.

OUR CHAMPION-SHIP

In the Philippines, champions are almost always thought of in terms of boxing, basketball, or track. The Apostle Paul imagined those scenarios too—at least the boxer and runner. Basketball wasn't played until 1891. At some point, most guys (and girls) on the basketball court have imagined themselves hitting the last-second shot to win the championship game. How many times have you seen a kid shadowboxing, pretending to be Manny Pacquiao? Others visualize winning a great race, exhausting their last drop of energy in a heroic sprint to the finish line. The few who have—at some point in their young lives—won championships often have difficulty getting over it. Have you ever heard a group of men reminiscing about a game they won 20 years ago?

I'm amazed by the frequency and the kind of conviction with which athletes pray for victory or point to the sky as a way of thanking "the man upstairs" for helping them defeat their opponents.

Whether it's a 3-km run or an ultramarathon, God doesn't care who comes first or last. Yes, I know God cares about every aspect of our lives, so let me put it this way: He does indeed care that we become champions, but not the way we care and not about the kind of champion this world celebrates. I think God is much more concerned about each of us becoming a champion as defined in the older and more traditional sense—one who stands in the gap for those in need; who becomes, in fact, their champion. As the Prophet Isaiah proclaimed: "It will become a sign and a witness to the Lord of hosts in the land of Egypt; for they will cry to the Lord because of oppressors, and He will send them a Savior and a Champion, and He will deliver them" (Isaiah 19:20, NASB).

In *100 Years from Now*, Pastor Steve Murrell (2013, 49) wrote about God as a champion of what Nicholas Wolterstorff has called the "quartet of the vulnerables"—the poor, the orphans, the sick, and the immigrants.

> Not only does God identify Himself with the most vulnerable and disenfranchised people, He is very sensitive to anyone who messes with them—those who oppress them, those who take advantage of them, those who do them injustice, or those who simply ignore them. The weaker and more defenseless the person, the more likely He is to assume the role as their protector, defender, and champion of their cause.

If God had a business card, it would look something like this:

God of Abraham, Isaac, and Jacob
Father to the Fatherless, Defender of Widows
Help to the Poor, Friend of the Alien
Championing the Cause of the Defenseless
Since the Creation of the World

LIKE FATHER, LIKE SON

Jesus Christ is the champion of our salvation. That's not just something that He did because of our helpless state. It seems to be an essential attribute of the Father being reflected in the Son.

During His earthly ministry, Jesus mirrored the heart of the Father as the defender of the needy. Again, Pastor Steve says in *100 Years from Now*:

> Jesus had a moral compass that guided and governed His words and His actions. He explained it in a short sentence. "Very truly I tell you, the Son can do nothing by himself; he can do only what He sees His Father doing, because whatever the Father does the Son also does" (John 5:19). In other words, when Jesus arrived on earth as the incarnate Son of God, He simply got busy doing the same things He had seen the Father doing. And what did the Son of God do? He preached the Gospel to the poor, including children and widows, helped a lot of sick people (Matthew 11:4-6), and reached out to the foreigners (the Romans and Samaritans). He condemned those who oppressed the needy, as well as those who simply did nothing to help (the rich man and Lazarus; the good Samaritan). He pronounced woes upon the Pharisees who were big on religion but not all that concerned about needy people. In all of these situations Jesus was showing us what the Father was really like by identifying with those in need and becoming their advocate.

Jesus is our deliverer, who became the substitutionary sacrifice for our sin. He is our redeemer, having given Himself as a ransom to purchase our freedom. And He is our great advocate, who continually pleads our case before the throne of God. Truly Jesus is the champion of our salvation.

I kept this in mind, and as a result I had never felt more energized, more passionate, or more empowered to run than I did on the *102-km Bataan Death March*. I wasn't running to become a champion; I was running because I realized there was somebody who stooped down to where we are to uphold us and make us great, who championed our cause (Psalm 18:35). Who are we not to do the same for those in need? What an opportunity we have to stoop down and make others great as well!

RUN50 CHALLENGE

Don't try to run the race set before you without a worthy aim or purpose. If discipleship is the ongoing act of becoming a disciple, then "champion-ship" is the ongoing act of becoming a champion. If you and I want to follow Christ, if we aspire to be like Him, to be conformed to His image, and to be empowered by His purpose, then we must become champions for something or someone. Conversely, if we are the champions of nothing or no one, we run our race "without aim." How then are we His disciples?

Strong people stand up for themselves, but stronger people stand up for others. Whose load are you carrying? For what or for whom are you standing in the gap? To what lengths will you go to champion the cause of those you serve? Would you do so only if it was convenient or cost very little? Do you only take up the cause of those who can reward you? Are you willing to become the champion of those who don't believe, for those who ridicule and persecute you?

So the *RUN50* challenge is this: Whose champion are you?

PASSION
RUNNING FOR THOSE WHO CAN'T RUN FOR THEMSELVES

Even at my age, I'm trying to improve. Never give up, no matter what. Even if you get last place—finish!

LOUIS ZAMPERINI
1936 Berlin Olympics, 5000 m
Subject of the book and movie, *Unbroken*

But I discipline my body and keep it under control, lest after preaching to others I myself should be disqualified.

1 CORINTHIANS 9:27

In 1942, it took about five days for the Filipino and American prisoners-of-war to complete the 102-km forced march from Mariveles to San Fernando. Only 54,000 of the 76,000 prisoners who began in Mariveles survived Camp O'Donnell. Created to commemorate this historical event, the *Bataan Death March 102K Ultra Marathon Race* in March 2011 was a grueling test of endurance, twice as long as anything I had attempted before. Every ultramarathon has a cutoff time. For this race, it was 18 hours. It began at 10:00 p.m. on Friday, and I crossed the finish line at 3:00 p.m. on Saturday, with 42 minutes to spare (17:17:39). Of the 142 runners who began the race, 112 finished. The rest either did not finish or were disqualified because they did not meet the cutoff time.

"Disqualified."

That's a word no ultramarathoner wants to hear. As the race goes on hour after hour, there's a growing sense of urgency among slower runners. *Pick up the pace or all the training will be for nothing.* Many runners press on to the point of exhaustion, even after time disqualifications. For them, quitting is just not an option. The Apostle Paul wrote, "So I do not run aimlessly; I do not box as one beating the air" (1 Corinthians 9:26). Our mission is urgent, and we don't have time or energy to waste. That's what I was thinking when I was tempted to divert from the *RUN50* course to visit my father's grave. Ultramarathoners in both natural and spiritual races have to remain focused on the finish line. The Apostle Paul continued, "But I discipline my body and keep it under control, lest after preaching to others I myself should be **disqualified**" (1 Corinthians 9:27).

Although one did not meet the cutoff time, the five of us finished the run together—championing the cause of the Real LIFE scholars.

EARLY MINISTRY

As a new believer, one of my first ministry assignments was to clean and prepare the basement of the Tandem Cinema in U-Belt for the service. Combating the foul odors that periodically revisited us was an ongoing project. My first leadership role was as a head usher. Some of the volunteer ushers and I would come in the early morning to clean the basement and set up chairs before the service. I remember arriving one morning and being hit with a particularly terrible smell that was difficult to identify—sewage, trash, or a dead animal—or a mixture of all three. We tracked the smell to a huge pile of garbage that had been dumped in front of the fan duct by the tenants next door. I was with Jojo Henson, a student from De La Salle University who I was helping disciple at that time. Together, we raked and shoveled the garbage and washed down the pavement, claiming victory over another day's challenge to holding church services in the Tandem Cinema basement. Looking back on those times, I've tried to imagine the ushers who served the early Christians meeting in the catacombs of Rome. With hundreds or thousands of people meeting in a cavern, they had to be dealing with odors.

My wife, Judy, and I met in 1984 during the original outreach led by Pastors Steve and Rice. My encounter with Christ at the rock-and-roll seminar was on June 23. Judy got saved three days later on June 26. We have been friends, brother and sister in Christ, since then. We were married seven years later on March 9, 1991. I was at that time a traveling evangelist, meaning I'd go from one province to another helping establish Victory churches. Judy served as a campus missionary in U-Belt. As a young married couple, we threw ourselves into ministry at Victory, serving as campus missionaries, children's pastors, Victory group leaders, associate pastors, and all the other things young Victory leaders did at that time.

Our daughter, Elle, came along 13 months later on April 25, 1992, and we were on the way to building our perfect little world. We wanted lots of sons and daughters who would become our little band of disciples. However, 12 years went by after Elle's birth without any new arrivals. We did everything we could to help God in the process, without success. By the time I was 39 and Judy was 37, we had pretty much concluded that the one we would exclusively devote ourselves to was Elle.

GRACE AND PATIENCE

Lessons on measuring out grace in abundance are not easily learned, especially for someone like me. That's a little frightening when I consider the words of Jesus, "For with the judgment you pronounce you will be judged, and with the measure you use it will be measured to you" (Matthew 7:2). I have not proven to be the most patient person. Those who've known me for many years would agree and exclaim, "Ha! Ferdie, when have you ever been patient?" Passion seems to come naturally to me; patience does not. People who are passionate about something often assume that others could do what they do if only they were just more dedicated, more focused, or more faithful. That's why, to those who tend to be melancholy, I've been known to say, "What's the matter? This is the day that the Lord has made! Why aren't you rejoicing?" And to those who grew weary and ran slowly, I issued a challenge: "Come on! Suck it up! Fatigue is only in your mind!"

Yep. As you can imagine, I've frequently had to make apologies.

The last 15 years have been an intense learning process for me. I've had to learn that every person has their own race to run, and for some, every step of the course laid out before them is extraordinarily difficult. I, for one, need to learn to extend grace and patience to slower runners.

Our son, Philip, has taught me a lot about love, grace, and patience.

JOHN PHILIP CABILING

In July 2003, we were shocked and overjoyed when Judy became pregnant with a son. I felt like old Abraham realizing that Sarah was pregnant with the promised son, Isaac. I had a hard time containing myself. In my imagination, I could see us running together, preaching the gospel, making disciples, shooting hoops. Note to self: if my son were to become the basketball player I never was, we'd have to get started early.

While I was having a grand old time with my plans and expectations, Judy was struggling through a difficult pregnancy. However, she gave birth without complications, and we were so thankful. I remember the first time I saw little Philip. I was watching him through the glass window in the viewing room. What an awesome feeling it was to see my newborn son! But when Philip turned his head, my heart sank. A dark purple birthmark covered the entire left half of his face.

"What is wrong? How can this be?" I began saying over and over in a panic. Philip's face looked half-painted, much like the face of Mel Gibson as William Wallace in the movie, *Braveheart*.

The doctor tried to emphasize the positive.

"He's a **healthy** little boy!" the doctor kept saying.

As I continued to look into my son's face, all I could think was, *Why did this happen to him?* We didn't know it then, but in the following days we would discover that this was the least of the challenges that would dominate Philip's young life. After numerous tests and consultations with the doctors, Philip was diagnosed with Type-1 Sturge-Weber Syndrome, a birth defect occurring in one out of every 50,000 newborns.

The prognosis of this particular type of Sturge-Weber is horrifyingly bleak—severe mental and physical retardation, glaucoma, frequent seizures beginning in infancy, and a host of other physical and cognitive difficulties, including a limited life expectancy. After learning all that, the facial birthmark now seemed no more serious than a mosquito bite.

We began firing questions at the doctors.

"What does this mean?"

"What can we do to fix this?"

"What will life be like for us and for our son?"

The doctors' answers were equally devastating—regular hospital visits, trips to the emergency room, more doctors, physical therapy sessions, special schools, and a never-ending regimen of powerful anticonvulsant drugs. It's hard to describe how devastated we were. I cried uncontrollably, while Judy remained stone silent. Pastor Steve and our friend, Pastor Joey Bonifacio, visited the hospital to be with us, but I was inconsolable. Judy was emotionally numb.

Contemplating the future for Philip and for us left me physically and emotionally exhausted. And yet, I was unable to sleep. I sat through the nights, staring at the array of tubes, wires, and monitor screens hooked up to my son. I would have loved to fall into a deep sleep as a momentary relief from the heavy burden of fear and worry. However, I felt a sense of guilt about it—like the disciples sleeping through the night of Jesus' betrayal. Could I not tarry one hour for my son?

Nurses would come in and out, writing on charts, taking his temperature, and changing IV bags. Around 3 o'clock one morning, a nurse came in and began going though her scheduled procedures. Seeing that I was awake, she began to talk as she did her work.

"Pastor, do you wonder why this has happened to you?" she asked. "Why was your son born with this condition?"

It seemed strange for a nurse to ask such a difficult question, and I'm pretty sure it was **not** a standard question hospital staff were supposed to ask all parents whose children were born with birth defects. Maybe it was her own personal question, something with which she was also struggling. Perhaps she was led by the

Holy Spirit to ask this question, a question that forced me to look at things from God's perspective.

The nurse continued her work until I finally replied, "You know, I was just asking God the same thing. But then when I looked at my son, I thought, *What if he was born into a family with no spiritual or emotional fortitude, or into a broken home?* I could not bear to think about what would have happened to him then.

"So," I continued, "instead of asking the question, 'Why me, Lord?' maybe I should ask, 'Why not me, Lord? Give him to me!'"

I didn't know it at the time, but that was the beginning of the long lesson God wanted to teach me about taking up the cause of those in need just as Christ stood in the gap for us. So often, the race we are called to run corresponds to the life lesson we are called to learn.

The nurse didn't respond but continued going about her duties. Finally, on the way out of the door, she said, "By the way, Pastor Ferdie, I go to your church. You were preaching the first time I attended, and you asked people to come forward to give their lives to Christ. And that's what I did that day!"

Once we got through the initial shock, Judy and I (mostly Judy) went into fix-it mode. We were determined to do the best we could for our son, maybe even (with all our best efforts) beat the odds associated with the depressing prognosis. That included trying to consult with Dr. Ben Carson. He was a renowned neurosurgeon at the Johns Hopkins Hospital in Baltimore, Maryland—a leading neurological hospital. He was also a Christian, and we had a mutual friend in Gordon Robertson, who at that time was in the Philippines. Pastor Joey asked Gordon if he could help connect us with Dr. Carson. Shortly afterward, Dr. Carson's secretary interviewed us. However, we didn't have the medical insurance required to be admitted to Johns Hopkins.

Instead, Philip was admitted to Cardinal Santos Medical Center in San Juan City, Metro Manila. At Cardinal Santos, even the smallest medical procedure, like finding a vein to draw blood or administer medication, was so complicated that it required an operation to insert an intravenous port. We encountered complication upon complication. Because of the challenge they had at that time in even finding a vein, stays in the hospital are still terrifying for us.

We went through three or four different anticonvulsant drugs trying to find one that would control the seizures that had already become regular occurrences in our day. The month we spent at the hospital was probably the most difficult we've ever been through. We continued asking our doctors a lot of questions: "What about this, what about that? What about the future?"

Finally, the doctors put it to us very bluntly. "It's going to be forever," they said. "Philip will always be this way, and there's really not much you can do about it."

In the following years, we adjusted to a radically different sense of normalcy. Judy went to Singapore to learn about alternatives to the powerful anticonvulsant drugs. After a couple of years of trying different medications, we were able to gradually wean Philip off all anticonvulsants. He's now 14 years old, and his seizures are less frequent, only occurring in extraordinary situations, such as when he has a cold or an allergy, when he gets too excited, or when he has high levels of stress. That sounds like a lot of exceptions, but things really have become better. We enrolled our son in a school for children with special needs. We focused on developing his life skills such as eating, walking, and getting dressed. The truth is, Philip has already exceeded his predicted life expectancy. And because of Philip, we learned not to worry or get stressed about the future but simply to enjoy the moments with him as they come. Philip's favorite moments are birthday celebrations. Now, birthday parties happen all the time at our house! We celebrate the birthdays of our immediate family, those of Judy's sister, her husband, and her two children—ten birthday parties in all, including one for their dog, Asher, and one for our dog, Selah.

We love our son immensely, notwithstanding all his challenges and regardless of all the effort he requires. And we love our daughter, Elle, just as much. After 12 years as an only child, she's had to make so many adjustments and live on the scant leftovers of her parents' attention. This seems so very unfair to her.

Elle did not at first grasp the seriousness of her brother's health condition. It was a tough time for her as well. She was 12 years old, going through adjustments as a preteen, trying to be her own person. Nonetheless, she was and still is an extraordinarily understanding and unselfish person. She has always tried to add as little additional weight to our shoulders as possible regarding her own needs and concerns. She contributed to the family by looking after Philip and accompanying Judy on her countless trips to the hospital. She brought her friends to our home to show them how she relates to her brother. It doesn't seem that Elle has ever been ashamed of Philip, though there have been many embarrassing moments. In the company of her friends, she always includes him. I've often wondered with amazement, *How is it that with her parents so intently focused on their special-needs son, we have a daughter who has turned out like this?*

These kinds of situations put a lot of pressure on families. In fact, many marriages break up and families fall apart because of the unrelenting stress. That's why Judy Cabiling is my greatest hero. As a wife and mother, she is a "dread champion" (Jeremiah 20:11, NASB) for my son and for our family. And she does it with such grace. We have our moments, of course, but the character and likeness of Christ demonstrated through my wife are simply extraordinary.

This has been a long and difficult run for Judy and me, but there have been a lot of great moments as well. Typically, I run in the evenings after work. That only happens if I'm very flexible. Running has to work around supper, bedtime, Philip's schedule, helping Judy, family time, and time with God. Sometime before the day is done, I'll get away for at least a quick 10 km.

One day, I came home early before dinner and began to put on my running shoes. Philip got excited and was trying to say something. I couldn't understand what his problem was or what he wanted. Judy finally stepped in to help.

"Ferdie, he saw you putting on your shoes. Philip wants to run with you."

How Judy can understand what Philip is trying to say is a great mystery to me. I think it's some kind of superpower—mother's intuition. We helped him put on his jogging pants and shoes. I held his hands as we shuffled along, leaving his little pushcart behind. In this way, Philip and I completed our first one-km "run" together around our village.

People in general tend to feel uncomfortable in the presence of a parent with their special-needs child. That's especially true if the parents are trying to deal with some emotional issue that's quickly becoming the center of attention. The uncomfortable feeling is probably one part sympathy and another part embarrassment for the parents—all of that and more being communicated in "the look" from bystanders. Far from being embarrassed or ashamed, I'm immensely proud of Philip, not only for our one-km run around the village, but for everything he does with such monumental effort. He's my other hero.

All of this has required some significant lifestyle changes for us. People at Victory Ortigas see Judy and Philip occasionally. For most of the last eight years, Judy has been rather invisible within the church. She's been "living in the moment" with our son. Lately, however, she has begun to carve out little pieces of her very precious time to lead a Victory group—reviving her own commitment to make disciples, including going through ONE 2 ONE with others and winning them to Christ.

So this is one of my greatest life lessons: every person (my son included) has his or her own race to run. And for some, every step of the course laid out for them is extraordinarily difficult. As a result, I've learned to extend grace to other runners.

QUITTING IS HIGHLY CONTAGIOUS

The *102-km Bataan Death March* was actually a prerequisite for an even greater challenge—the *160-km Bataan Death March*. The stretch from Mariveles to San Fernando was only part of the original march in 1942. When they reached the San Fernando railway station, the prisoners were jam-packed into boxcars and transported by rail to Capas, Tarlac, then forced to march another 14 km to Camp O'Donnell.

The *160-km Bataan Death March* was coming up in February 2012, a run from the 00-km historical marker in Mariveles all the way to Camp O'Donnell with an additional five-km run back down to the finish line at the Bataan Death March Memorial. Three months after our 102-km run in 2011, I began preparing for the even more challenging 160-km run, which had three stages of at least 50 km each. I was the only one from our group of runners who intended to enter the 160-km marathon, but the others joined me anyway in the preparatory runs. The first was the *PAU-Fort Magsaysay 60K Ultra Run* in July 2011 (09:10:07). The second was the *Western Pangasinan 65K Run* from Bolinao to Sual in August 2011 (10:23:45). The third was a 50-km ultramarathon from Tagaytay to Nasugbu in September 2011 (06:34:21).

We didn't have sponsors or pledges. We were all just putting in mileage, the others helping me prepare for the upcoming 160-km run. That doesn't mean that they were recreational runs. Ultramarathoners tend to be ultra-serious about how the race is organized and how runners conduct themselves. There's a list of strong recommendations for full-length marathons and ultramarathons, unless clearly stated otherwise. Here are a few:

Cheaters are automatically disqualified.

Every runner must have a support vehicle.

Runners who finish after the cutoff time for each leg are disqualified.

Runners must stay on the left side of the road.

Runners must submit medical certificates.

Runners shall ask permission to display corporate sponsors.

Race bibs should always be visible.

Runners should wear appropriate attire for the event.

Runners cannot go inside a support vehicle.

Although the list of rules is long, every runner is thankful for each of them because they were written with the runners' safety in mind.

All five of us signed up to run the entire *65-km Western Pangasinan* run in August 2011. Alden Meneses and I agreed to run and finish together. There are a lot of unpredictables in an ultramarathon. When five guys agree to follow a particular race strategy and run at a precise pace, the chances of something going wrong multiply with each additional runner. At the 20-km mark, I began to have stomach cramps that seemed to be increasing as I ran.

"Alden, you go on ahead," I said. "I'll catch up."

So much for staying together for the whole race. I slowed down a bit, hoping my stomach would cooperate with our race plans. Alden pressed on ahead until I lost sight of him. At the 33-km mark, I came upon our team's van. When I reached in to grab a bottle of water, there was Alden, sitting next to the driver. I was dumbfounded.

"Alden, why are you sitting here?"

"Bro, I quit."

"WHAT?! Why have you quit the race?"

Alden replied, "It's hot, I'm dehydrated, and I feel weak. Besides, we're not running for Real LIFE scholars. This is just a practice run."

I was shocked. We don't quit races until we're finished. The stomach cramps, however, were still bothering me. And, yes, he was right about not running for a cause this time.

Maybe it's okay if I quit too, I began thinking to myself. I was also tired, my stomach cramps were not going away, and we were not running to raise money for anyone. *It's hard to think of a good reason to keep running today.* I sat down on a stool to rest. After a few moments, I began staring down at my legs. My thoughts went immediately to my son, Philip, struggling to complete that one km around the village with me.

I became angry with myself and thought, *I've got two good legs, but my son can barely walk. I have to run for those who can't.* Looking around to be sure that none of my crew members were watching, I began to cry. Then I jumped up, maybe a little too quickly. I was dizzy and wobbling for a few moments, but I regained my balance and resumed the run—fully determined to complete the race I had begun. I limped on for the remaining 32 km to the finish.

IRRATIONAL PASSION

Several years have passed since that particular race. Alden and I still joke about what happened on the Western Pangasinan road in 2011. The story sounds crazy as I retell it. In his dehydrated condition, with no cause or pledge on the line, Alden had made the right decision to quit. With my stomach cramps, I probably should have quit too. But God was teaching me something I wouldn't have learned otherwise.

Trained as a civil engineer, my first inclination is to measure with great precision the impact of one thing upon another. It's easy to understand the impact of running to raise funds for Real LIFE scholars. The runners secure their pledges, run the race, report the mileage, collect the funds, and give it all to Real LIFE. But to say I'm simply running for those who can't run for themselves doesn't make a lot of sense. In other words—how, precisely, is my running benefiting those who can't run? That's not an easy question to answer. It's the idea of identification and substitution. Christ identified with our inabilities and, consequently, became our substitutionary sacrifice. Don't misunderstand me—I'm not equating my sense of running for Philip with Christ's suffering for us. What I'm saying is this: I've so identified with my son, with his struggle, and with his suffering that I cannot help but make the connection between my ability and Philip's disability. It's hard to explain, but it's a result of loving someone so intensely that you share the burden of their suffering and limitations. It makes no difference if pledges or prizes are on the line.

On Day 17 of *RUN50*, I had arrived in the city of Catbalogan. I was sitting down, having finished my 50-km run that day, waiting for the officials to emerge from the city hall to begin the program. I was mentally gearing up to preach the gospel and pray for them all.

While I was resting, a middle-aged woman seated next to me touched me on the shoulder, looked straight into my eyes, and said, "Thank you for running for me."

"What do you mean?" I replied.

"You said on your website, 'I run for those who can't run for themselves.' Look at me."

She showed me her legs, deformed and lifeless because of polio. Then, with a big smile, she said, "When I die someday and go to heaven, do you know what I'll do first? I'm going to run!"

She understood what it meant for someone to identify with her inabilities just as I had with Philip's. It turned out that she was a successful obstetrician-gynecologist and the wife of the pastor who had welcomed us to the city. My brief conversation with her really made an impact on me. It seems that my substitutionary run and her handicap connected us powerfully, and I was grateful that she understood me.

The race that God set before Judy, Elle, Philip, and me has not been an easy one, and we would never wish it on anyone else. We have, however, learned a lot about grace, patience, love, and identifying with those in need. And that has been a good thing.

RUN50 CHALLENGE

Hours before His crucifixion, Jesus was approached by a woman with an alabaster vial of costly perfume (Matthew 26:6-13, NASB). As she began to pour it upon Jesus' head, the disciples became indignant, saying, "Why this waste?" By their estimation, the gift, though very passionate, didn't make a lot of sense. The disciples even suggested a more effective means of stewardship, saying,

"This perfume could be sold for a high price and the money given to the poor." Jesus corrected them, stating that the woman was doing something so meaningful that wherever the gospel would be preached, what she had done would be remembered. Though the gift didn't make much sense, it was an act of passion.

Like this woman, we, as followers of Christ, value things differently. As a result, we may do strange things that seem irrational to the world. When was the last time you did something out of passion that seemed irrational or a waste of time and effort to others but was simply a response to God's love, grace, and patience?

KEEP THE FAITH

07 PREPARATION
BUILDING THE CASE FOR THE HOPE THAT IS IN YOU

08 YOUR RACE
RUNNING FOR YOUR LIFE

09 YOUR CALLING
THE RACE THAT IS SET BEFORE YOU

10 YOUR FOCUS
FIXING YOUR EYES ON JESUS

11 YOUR VISION
KEEPING PACE WITH AN EXPANDING STEWARDSHIP

12 YOUR FAITH
LEARNING FROM YOUR HEROES

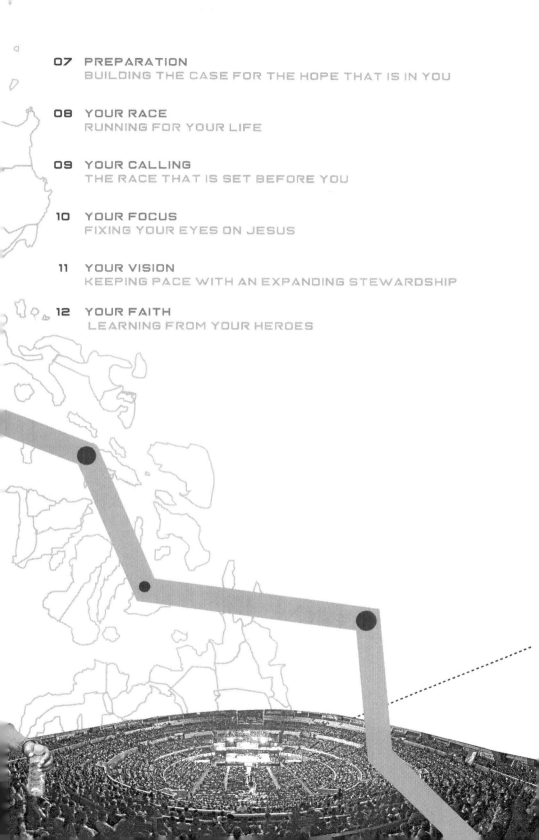

07
PREPARATION
BUILDING THE CASE FOR THE HOPE THAT IS IN YOU

The will to win means nothing without the will to prepare.

JUMA IKANGAA
1989 New York City Marathon, First Place

If you have raced with men on foot and they have worn you out, how can you compete with horses? If you stumble in safe country, how will you manage in the thickets by the Jordan?

JEREMIAH 12:5 (NIV)

As I crossed the finish line at the *160-km Bataan Death March* in 2012, the race organizer, retired two-star general Jovie Narcise, gave me a big enthusiastic hug. My combined run time for the three stages of the *160-km Bataan Death March* was 28 hours, 44 minutes, and 46 seconds. The last 13 km of that race had been extraordinarily difficult and took more out of me than I realized. I probably wouldn't have completed that race without my pacers, Alden Meneses and Jerome Bautista.

Before the general awarded the medals, early finishers had to stand aside and wait as other runners completed the race. That's standard procedure at most races, and it's much like what the old covenant (Old Testament) saints are doing right now. Having finished their own races (with great suffering, faith, and endurance), they now comprise that "great cloud of witnesses" (Hebrews 12:1). As I stood with the other runners and cheered for the late finishers, people began to ask me, "Pastor Ferdie, are you going to run again next year?" At that point, I was exhausted and in a lot of pain.

"Maybe this is it for me," I said. "I've finished the most incredible and demanding 160-km race. I think I can spend the rest of my life bragging."

After that race, my body was hurting all over, and I had big blisters on both feet. I took time off from running because the healing process of my feet and muscles was taking much longer than it had after the 102-km race in 2011. The blisters and general soreness made it so hard to use stairs that I slept downstairs on a folding bed. Going to the office was something I looked forward to every day, except for the fact that I had to put on socks and shoes. That was not only painful, it also hindered the recovery process. Every evening, I would return from work and almost immediately go to sleep on my folding bed. My motivation to continue running was registering zero. The tank was empty. This *Bataan Death March* had taken more out of me than any race I had previously run—much more than I had thought it would. I had all but concluded that with a 160-km race on my record, it was time to call it quits.

That all changed in May 2012 at the three-month mark of my slow recovery. I wasn't running, but I did continue to keep up with what other runners were doing. One morning, as I was reading some articles online, I came across a blog post by a priest, Father

Amado Picardal—"Father Picx." He was celebrating the one-year anniversary of his run across the Philippines in April 2011.

I was astonished at the feat, just as I had been the first time I heard about people running 102 km in the *Bataan Death March*.

A person can actually do that? I thought.

There were some photos of the towns and villages the priest had passed through, as well as daily posts about his 57-day run for peace and reconciliation in the Philippines. I don't remember ever thinking, *Ferdie, you cannot run across the Philippines.* It had just never occurred to me that anyone would. I found out later that six people had done it:

Cesar Guarin	Zamboanga to Baguio in 1983
Father Robert Reyes	Mindanao in 1996, Visayas in 1997, and Luzon in 1998
Joy Rojas	Davao to Pagudpud in 2005
Mat Macabe	Davao to Pagudpud in 2005
Father Amado "Picx" Picardal	Davao to Aparri in 2011
Cenen "Mac" Milan Jr.	Davao to Manila in 2012

Two of the trans-Philippine runners were priests—Father Picx was the second, preceded by the activist priest, Father Robert Reyes. Of course, both wore running gear, but it would be rather amusing to imagine a priest in his hooded robe and sandals running across the Philippines. Father Reyes had started, stopped, and completed the transnational run in a little over two years. Nonetheless, they had all locked in on the vision and completed it. And if a couple of priests could complete such a run, why not the Running Pastor?

I had not been practicing my stand-in-the-gap "championship" at a very high level (i.e. championing the cause of the poor, the weak, and the disenfranchised). In fact, I'd been licking my wounds, hobbling around, and feeling sorry for myself. Reading Father Picx's blog, however, was like a shot of adrenalin. Suddenly, I felt a renewed surge of vision and faith. It's not that I was lacking vision and faith for ministry or that my passion to preach the gospel had waned. I had lost my sense of purpose in running after completing that ultramarathon. I had run my greatest race; what else did I have to prove? Yes, I could continue bragging about my accomplishments, but I had always been forward-thinking as a runner, always preparing for the next great race. I felt like a professional athlete trying to adjust to retirement or like one of the old men reminiscing about their glory days on the court or in the ring. I was surprised at how quickly the celebration of my finish in the *160-km Bataan Death March* was losing its significance. The Apostle Paul wrote about runners training for a race in order to "receive a perishable wreath" (1 Corinthians 9:25). Very true, and mine was fading fast.

But Father Picx's blog opened my eyes to new possibilities. *If a priest could do this to raise awareness for peace,* I said to myself, *why couldn't I run across the Philippines for Real LIFE scholars?* It's amazing how when others step out and lead the way, the most outrageous ideas seem very possible—things that you would never before have considered undertaking.

I began counting in my head—*2013, 2014, 2015 . . . In 2015, I will be 50 years old.* I couldn't wait to tell Judy about my new vision—to celebrate my 50th birthday with a 2,000-km run across the Philippines. She was probably tired of my moping around the house, battling over the decision to quit or continue. She explains her reaction this way:

> Being married to Ferdie for 21 years, I am used to his crazy ideas and out-of-this-world declarations. Here was another one. He told me that he had read about a priest who ran across the Philippines and announced that he was inspired to do it for his 50th birthday. In my mind I was thinking, *Here we go again. First the* 102-km Bataan Death March, *then the 160 km that he's been trying to recover from for three months. Now he wants to run across the Philippines!*
>
> I replied to my excited husband, "Can't you just celebrate your 50th birthday like a normal person? Does it have to be such a big, dangerous, on-the-ragged-edge type of celebration?"
>
> I didn't wait for him to answer. I just gave a deep sigh and surrendered to the fact that once Ferdie got an idea in his head, it was almost impossible to get it out. I concluded that whether I supported him or not, he was going to do it. So I might as well be there for him.

The next day, I called to set up a meeting with Titus Salazar, a level-four running coach who was also a member of Victory Ortigas.

"Titus," I said excitedly, "I read about a priest who ran all the way across the Philippines—from the southern tip of Mindanao to the northern edge of Luzon, over 2,000 km! Can you believe it? I'm going to do that too, and I'm going to raise money for Real LIFE scholars. Will you be my coach?"

"Are you sure you really want to do this, Pastor Ferdie?" he asked, measuring my resolve.

"Yes, I am, and I'll celebrate my 50th birthday along the way." Again I asked, "Will you be my coach?"

"Sure, Pastor Ferdie. I'd be happy to coach you." Then, as if he had set the countdown clock into motion and it was already ticking, he said, "We must get started right away. We have to begin our preparations."

My first inclination was to call the run across the Philippines "Cross Country PH 2015." After nursing that idea for a while, I changed it to "Run Across PH." Still, that wasn't quite the title I was looking for. I gathered some volunteers from Victory to brainstorm—Elisa Yu, Layla Lopez, Eden Ilagan, and Janelle Pacete. Finally, Janelle suggested "RUN50" because it was easy to remember, the tentative schedule was to run for less than 50 days at 50 km a day, and I would be celebrating my 50th birthday during the run.

We asked Bok Jamlang to begin designing a logo. I was locked in on the vision, and now it had a name—*RUN50*.

THE SALAZAR RULE OF DISCIPLINE

I'd been running since the early 1980s, putting in thousands of hours on the road. I placed 83rd out of 112 finishers in the *102-km Bataan Death March* in 2011 (17:17:39) and 32nd out of 53 finishers in the *160-km Bataan Death March* in 2012 (28:44:46). I considered myself to be in excellent physical condition, with a lot of race experience to my credit. What I expected from Coach Salazar was just more of the same encouragement that I had been getting from my pacers and running mates. However, I had significantly underestimated what it was going to be like training for a 2,180-km race with a level-four running coach. Coach Salazar turned out to not only be a race strategist but also the demanding taskmaster I needed. He also became my chief encourager.

Every Monday during my day off, we would go to the PhilSports Complex track oval early in the morning to run while my family was still asleep. I thought I knew a lot about running, but Coach Salazar started from the beginning with lesson #1. On that first day, he told me, "Pastor Ferdie, you run; I'll watch."

When I returned, Coach Salazar was shaking his head as he pronounced the diagnosis. "Pastor Ferdie, you're wasting energy. You need to change the way you run."

I was thinking, *I just finished a 160-km run, and you're telling me I'm not doing it right?*

"From now on, this is how you will run," he said. Over time and against my objections, I had to get used to a new running style. He was right, though. He taught me how to conserve energy and prevent injuries. As it eventually became natural to me, I thought, *Oh, how I wish I had known this in that last grueling race!*

Coach Salazar engaged me in a war against anything and everything that would stand in the way of finishing my run across the Philippines. That also applied to my diet. I avoided eating meat, except for fish—a lot of fish! I ate vegetables, salad, rice, and root crops like *kamote* (sweet potato). I avoided staying up late so I could get a full night's rest before running early each morning. I would saturate my soul with God's Word by listening to it on my long morning runs. Coach Salazar was persistent about running techniques, diet, and other lifestyle aspects of preparation for a race. However, one of the most significant obstacles to actually completing *RUN50* was my self-image as a runner, and my coach worked on it relentlessly.

"You're a world-class athlete!" he would tell me over and over. You can't be that kind of an athlete until you see yourself that way. Coach Salazar was not content in merely hearing me acknowledge his vision or even repeat it back to him. He felt it essential that this image be imprinted deeply into my way of thinking.

In an earlier chapter, I wrote about my college days when I began to see myself as a runner. Running, for me, came to be more than merely something I did or forced myself to do—it was a part of who I was. And that made all the difference then. However, my self-image as a runner has had to grow to keep pace with my increasing vision. In college I began to see myself as a runner, then progressively as a long-distance runner, an ultramarathoner, and a finisher in the *Bataan Death March*. In Coach Salazar's way of thinking, my self-image as a runner was about 2,020 km short of the 2,180-km objective of *RUN50*.

Filipinos are not big on self-promotion; instead, we tend to self-deprecate. It's a common characteristic of our Filipino culture, while essential to our Christian culture is its counterpart, humility. As both a Filipino and a Christian, I'm not accustomed to talking or thinking more of myself than I ought.

The writer of Hebrews exhorted his audience to "throw off everything that hinders" as they run their race (Hebrews 12:1, NIV). As relentless as Coach Salazar was about attacking anything that would hinder me from finishing my race, he was equally persistent at encouraging me and building my confidence. He would talk to me and about me to others in the most extreme terms—like I was an Olympic gold-medal contender or a world-class athlete. Every time he did that, I got the same feeling I had back in 1984 when, in the wake of my utter failure at presenting the gospel, Pastor Steve announced to everyone, "Ferdie is the best evangelist I have ever been with on campus!" I'm so thankful for all the people who have encouraged me in both my physical and spiritual races. I'm equally thankful for the Victory group leaders who are coaching young believers in the same way.

Coach Salazar also challenged me on my long-term vision as a "world-class athlete."

"See those older guys on the track?" he said. "They walk instead of run because they started late. But you're a lifetime runner, and you're not going to be like that, Ferdie. My goal for you is that you'll still be running well into your 70s."

"Is that really possible?" I asked.

"Oh, yes. It's very possible."

And such were Coach Titus Salazar's mental and physical rules of discipline.

Father Picx's blog renewed my vision in a way that seemed to pull me out of the emotional exhaustion in which I'd been stuck for months. I became hyper-focused on the possibility of a run across the Philippines. The sore muscles didn't bother me anymore. I immediately sent Father Picx a Facebook message: "I read your blog about the anniversary of your run across the Philippines. Can

I meet with you to hear more of your story and get some tips on how you did it?"

Father Picx answered immediately, "You can visit me at my CBCP (Catholic Bishops' Conference of the Philippines) office." Due to challenges with my schedule, I never made it to his office; but we communicated with a barrage of Facebook messages.

I eventually met with all six of those who had run across the Philippines: Father Reyes in the early days of my preparation and the other five in the last months before *RUN50*. On August 15, 2015, Elle and I finally met Father Picx. I asked him for his advice for my own run across the Philippines, which was scheduled to begin in less than a month. He advised me to keep things simple as I met people along the way, to endure and resist the temptation to quit, and most of all, to appreciate the whole country as I ran across it—the beauty of our people and our native land.

PRACTICAL PREPARATIONS

Preparing for *RUN50* was an intense training process lasting over three years. However, you can't engage in real training without joining real races. Consequently, from the birth of the *RUN50* vision in 2012 to the *RUN50* starting point in 2015, I ran many and increasingly longer races.

In 2013, I ran the *160-km Bataan Death March* for the second time and placed 21st out of 43 finishers (28:44:40). The first run had wiped me out for three months. There are three segments in that race—50 km in the first stage, 52 km in the second stage, and 58 km in the final stage. My transnational *RUN50* averaged about 50 km per day for 44 run days, only resting on Sundays. So the 2013 repeat of the *160-km Bataan Death March* was a second preview of what the first three days of *RUN50* would be like. God's questions to Jeremiah might have applied to me in this situation: "If you have raced with men on foot and they have worn you out, how can you compete with horses? If you stumble in safe country, how will you manage in the thickets by the Jordan?" (Jeremiah 12:5, NIV).

Good questions, and the answer in my own situation was encouraging. As a result of Coach Salazar's training, the 160-km race was nothing like the year before—neither the run nor the recovery. Though I only beat my previous time by six seconds, I recovered in about a week. I hadn't reached the place where I could have run another 50 km in a fourth stage, but it was valuable experience and a significant confidence builder. I felt myself making progress.

THE HAZARD OF RUNNING OFF-COURSE

My goal was to run the *160-km Bataan Death March* for a third time in 2014 and then the *RUN50* across the Philippines in 2015. However, I heard that General Jovie Narcise was organizing a new and even more challenging race—a 250-km run through the mountains from Manila to Baguio. It was to be a three-stage run. Stage one would begin at Rizal Park in Manila and go through Caloocan and Bulacan along the MacArthur Highway to Dau, Pampanga—a total of 90 km. Stage two would cover another 90 km from Dau to Urdaneta City, Pangasinan. Stage three would be 70 km from Urdaneta to Rizal Park, Baguio City. That seemed like such a long run, but if I was serious about running 2,180 km in 50 days, I needed a greater test for myself. So I chose to enter the *Manila to Baguio 250K Ultra Marathon Race*. Thirty-seven runners began the race; 24 finished within the 50-hour cutoff time. I was not one of those 24.

In Chapter 2, I wrote about one of the hazards that will keep a runner from finishing his or her race—going off-course.

On the same day as the *250-km Manila-Baguio race*, there was a strategic planning meeting at Victory. Kevin York (Executive Director of Every Nation Churches and Ministries), Rachel Ong (CEO of Rohei and an organizational consultant of Victory), and Pastor Steve had all flown into Manila. Since I love my job and would very much like to keep it, there was no way I would miss this meeting or even consider being excused. I called General Narcise and asked if I could begin the race 12 hours later—at 1:00 p.m. rather than at 1:00 a.m. He had known me from previous races, and I guess he sensed my sincerity. He agreed to my request, with the understanding that I would call him from the starting line in Manila, take a photo, and keep track of my time. Having done all that, on Friday afternoon, my team and I set off from Manila for the first stage of the Manila-Baguio race.

Almost immediately, I encountered three problems. First of all, I had an allergic reaction to the sunscreen with which I had covered myself. It's hard to stay focused on the race when you're itching all over, especially in places you can't reach to scratch. Secondly, since the first two stages of the run didn't require pacers, I was running alone. The third problem was the late start. I reached Malolos, Bulacan around 7:00 p.m., and it was already dark. With no guide, my support vehicle went straight toward Nueva Ecija instead of turning left toward Pampanga. I followed my support vehicle, not knowing that with every pace, I was getting further and further from the stage-one finish line.

Two and a half km later I saw my support vehicle stop and my crew members walking toward me.

They told me we were on the wrong road.

"Pastor Ferdie, we are so sorry. We're supposed to be going to Dau, Pampanga, but we're on the road to Nueva Ecija."

"How could this happen?" I started to say. But also, how could I be angry? They were volunteers from church, and I was their pastor. They were beating themselves up pretty badly as it was. No need for me to add to their misery.

"Ah, it's okay, it's okay," I said. "It's part of running. You get lost sometimes."

Since we had run several km in the wrong direction and I was already past the 70-km mark, they encouraged me to get in the van to ride back to the crossroad where we should have turned left.

"No," I said. "If I do that, I'll be disqualified. That's the rule in running. We'll just run back to the turn."

After that was said, no one mentioned the fact that we were running 12 hours behind all the other teams and that no one would know if we simply rode back to where we had gone off-course.

We got back on the right road and continued on to Dau, but time was running out. Since we were running alone, I called the team in the van and asked them to look for a marker. At nine minutes after the 16-hour cutoff, I called the general, ended up speaking to someone else, and related what had happened. I was told that the other runners were on the second stage, running towards Urdaneta, and that it was impossible for me to catch up with them. It didn't really matter. The time limit for the first 90-km stage was 16 hours, and I was already at 16:11:00. My official time for the race was DNF (Did Not Finish).

When we finally reached Dau, I rested for a while. Then I took the van to the second-stage finish line to speak to the general. I apologized, explaining that I had exceeded the 16-hour time limit and was therefore disqualified. However, maybe as a reward for my honesty, the general gave me the pink finisher's shirt anyway. It took me several days to get over the allergic reaction to the sunscreen.

Three weeks later, we returned to the 90-km post in Dau, Pampanga with Pastor Jonathan Navalta of Victory Tabuk to run the second stage. We ran the 90 km to Urdaneta, Pangasinan, completing that leg.

After a week, I went back to the 180-km post at Rosales, Pangasinan with Pastor Junn Besana, and we started our run toward Baguio City. As we were running along the MacArthur Highway in Pozzorubio, Pangasinan, a busload of upcoming pastors and church planters from Victory were on their way to an outreach in Baguio. They saw us and started cheering. That was a needed boost for our tired bodies. We finished the last stage at the 250-km post in Rizal Park, Baguio City, at 5:37 p.m. on March 8, 2014 (15:08:00)—in four weeks instead of three days.

During the long hours of an ultramarathon, there's a lot of time to think and talk to yourself. I remembered my father's simple code of ethics: "Bong, finish what you start!" When I finally completed the race, Pastor Junn Besana took a photo of me kissing the 250-km mark.

AFTERTHOUGHT

Despite the late start, sunburn, allergic reaction, wrong turn, and subsequent disqualification, I'm glad I entered that race, and I'm even more thankful that I went back and finished it. It taught me what a 250-km run through the mountains was like. If I doubled that, it would be the distance across the island of Mindanao. Visayas is just 800 km long, and Luzon is over a 1,000 km long. So in my head I divided Luzon into two parts: Matnog, Sorsogon to Manila (500 km) and Manila to Aparri, Cagayan (500 km).

I was not just preparing my legs for *RUN50*. With each new challenge, the foundation of my faith was strengthened—that is to say, the evidence underlying my crazy step of faith was growing more and more solid. The vision for *RUN50* was also becoming more and more clearly defined. I was reminded of the story of David, the young shepherd boy, as he listened to the challenge from the nine-foot-tall Goliath. Goliath, the champion of the Philistines, was calling for someone to come out and fight in a winner-take-all contest. Those who lost would become slaves of the winners and possibly fade away as a forgotten nation.

While David seemed no match for Goliath, he leaned back on the faith-building experiences that had prepared him for that moment. He said to King Saul, "Your servant has killed both the lion and the bear; and this uncircumcised Philistine will be like one of them, since he has taunted the armies of the living God" (1 Samuel 17:36, NASB). That's why David took Goliath's challenge personally and stepped forward to champion the cause of Israel.

TWENTY-MILE MARCHING

Best-selling author and researcher Jim Collins (2011) gives an outstanding example of the virtue of steady plodding in his book, *Great by Choice*. In 1911, two groups of explorers, one led by Roald Amundsen and the other by Robert Scott, embarked on a race to be the first to reach the South Pole. Neither team knew where the other was or how close they were to reaching the goal.

Amundsen's strategy was to march 20 miles (mi) each day—regardless of the weather or the terrain—and then stop. If the temperature dipped to 40 degrees below zero, the Amundsen team marched approximately 20 mi. If there was a blizzard, they would still march 20 mi. If the weather was warm, the winds were calm, and the going easy—again, they marched 20 mi. Twenty miles was always the objective, no more, no less. Even when an extended march of 25 mi would have enabled them to reach the South Pole faster, Amundsen stuck to his practice of 20-mi marching.

In contrast, Robert Scott marched with his team as far as they could go on calm days. If the terrain was difficult, he shortened the day's march, and when the weather was bad, they remained in their tents. Robert Scott and his team never made it back from the South Pole. Their expedition was plagued by all sorts of calamities, most of them self-inflicted. Scott and several members of his team starved to death or died from exposure in the Antarctic.

Even if your progress seems slow, steady plodding and fanatical consistency have their benefits. Bill Gates, cofounder of Microsoft, is quoted as saying, "We greatly overestimate what we can accomplish in one year but greatly underestimate what we can accomplish in a decade."

There were sections of the 2,180-km course of *RUN50* from Maasim to Aparri that were mountainous, hot, and dangerous. There were also parts that were flat and cool. And there were times when I was running with or without pain. As an ultramarathoner I am by habit (what you might call) a steady plodder. Our general *RUN50* objective was the same every day—50 km, no more, no less. It was a practical application of Amundsen's 20-mi marching strategy.

RUN50 CHALLENGE

People, even those who are zealous to serve God, put limitations on their ability to envision the future. This happens for several reasons:

1. They are unwilling to lock in on a vision that goes beyond themselves. Having a vision for your own career or position is not necessarily a bad thing and individuals will pursue those dreams with great persistence. However, a challenge to become a servant and champion of others often forces you to take great steps of faith not necessarily of your own choosing—into battles with the Goliaths of your own generation. Championing the cause of others in the name of Christ is far more rewarding than all the riches of this world and the most meaningful thing you'll ever do.

2. They tend to envision what they might do or what race they might be called to run based on their *current* abilities—how much they can endure or how fast they can go right now. Juma Ikangaa, who won first place in the *1989 New York City Marathon,* once said, "The will to win means nothing without the will to prepare."

3. They place limitations on themselves because of their low sense of self. One of the most important things Coach Salazar taught me was to see myself as a world-class athlete, even when that was far from a realistic estimation of my running ability. In a spiritual sense, it is seeing myself with eyes of faith—as God sees me. One of the greatest things Victory group leaders can do for those they are in discipleship with is to see them with eyes of faith, and encourage them as Pastor Steve, Coach Salazar, and others have done for me.

4. Their ability to accept God's calling as their own is hindered by a short-term perspective. They see their race as a 100-meter (m) dash rather than an ultramarathon. Nothing is wrong with running fast, but the prime directive is to finish. Preparing for *RUN50* was, in one sense, an intense three-year process. But in another sense, it had taken 30 years.

The *RUN50* challenge is this: Are you putting limitations on your ability to envision the future God has for you?

08

YOUR RACE
RUNNING FOR YOUR LIFE

I had as many doubts as anyone else. Standing on the starting line, we're all cowards.

ALBERTO SALAZAR
1982 Boston Marathon, Winner

Therefore, since we are surrounded by so great a cloud of witnesses, let us also lay aside every weight, and sin which clings so closely, and let us run with endurance the race that is set before us, looking to Jesus, the founder and perfecter of our faith, who for the joy that was set before him endured the cross, despising the shame, and is seated at the right hand of the throne of God. Consider him who endured from sinners such hostility against himself, so that you may not grow weary or fainthearted.

HEBREWS 12:1-3

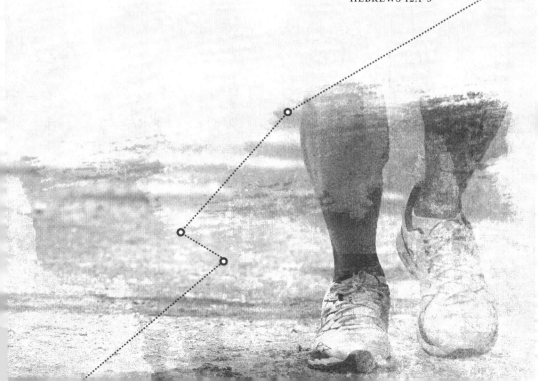

There's nothing particularly spiritual about working out, eating healthy, or running like a crazy man to stay in shape. Of course, our bodies are God's temples, but people go through those same exercises and diets not due to a fear of God or concern for "His temple." However, men and women who are filled with a vision for the great work in which they are engaged commonly make healthy lifestyles a priority. God's calling is not simply a job to them—it's a life's mission from which they have no intention of retiring. They're deeply committed to pursuing the cause and running their race with as much energy as possible, all the way to the finish line.

As I was approaching Day 1 of *RUN50*, I felt the waves of excitement getting stronger and stronger. I'd been training for this particular run for three years, but in a broader sense, I'd been in training for much of my adult life. I had not worked out the particulars of what all that training was leading to, but in time, the course fell into place. We're all in training for some purpose— some race to which we have been called or have yet to be called to. Some races are harder than others; some are celebrated by cheering followers; some are obscure courses like the long lonely stretches on the Maharlika Highway (also known as the Pan-Philippine Highway)—sometimes with just one other pacer running alongside. Sometimes you run all by yourself.

It's easy for me to wonder, *What's the purpose of all the self-inflicted pain and suffering I'm going through?* When training for ultramarathons, this thought goes through my mind a lot. But preparation is the point of any kind of training—whether for your head, your heart, your finances, or your body. Putting in mileage is short-term pain for long-term gain. Still the question is inescapable. If you're not clear about the *for what* or the *for whom*, when trying to prepare yourself for what might become an extraordinary calling, your resolve will often wither like the sower's seed in the hot sun (Matthew 13:5,6).

Unfortunately, many lose heart in training because they cannot see where God's calling might lead them, or simply have not put their trust in the One who's calling. A few will keep accumulating mileage, training for a race they've never even contemplated. I like what the great American president, Abraham Lincoln, said during his early days, when it seemed that he would remain a seemingly insignificant frontier lawyer: "I will prepare, and someday my chance will come." And come, it surely did.

Let me put a finer point on what I mean to say. I love to run; I've done it all of my adult life. But my recreational fun runs could never have sufficiently prepared me for the race I eventually felt the Lord had set before me. As the calling became more clearly defined, so did the training. In fact, the training had to shift into a higher gear to match the calling.

THE LAUNCH

The *RUN50* course we laid out began in the municipality of Maasim on the southern tip of Sarangani and was to conclude in the municipality of Aparri, Cagayan at the northernmost tip of Luzon. Throughout the 50 days, we arranged for me to end each Saturday's run in a city where we have a Victory church or in its vicinity. That way, I could take a break on Sundays to preach. Of the eight Sundays in the run, I preached once in a Baptist church, once in a Methodist church, and at six Victory churches.

This itinerary led to running for 50 km each day for 44 days. That, and my 50th birthday on Day 3 (September 8), were why we settled on the name *RUN50* for my 2,180-km run.

In September 2015, as we were getting ready to kick off *RUN50*, we were all packed up and about to head to the starting point at the southernmost tip of the Philippines. I kept saying, "This is it! We're finally ready to go."

If your mental picture of the starting line for our daily 50 km is a group of runners milling around drinking coffee at sunrise, your picture is about three to four hours behind. My average daily run time was nine hours, and the typical start time was around 2:00 a.m. We crawled out of bed four hours before sunrise each day after running more than the course of a full marathon the day before, and the day before that, and the day before that, and so on. Let's just say that I've done easier things. But let's also say that many have done and are doing much harder things.

Such difficulties in life abound, and there was never a more difficult task attempted than rebuilding the walls of Jerusalem after the people of Judah returned from 70 years of captivity in Babylon. They were surrounded by hostile forces and were forced to work in a combat zone with a weapon in one hand and a construction tool in the other. That was the situation to which Nehemiah was called, and it would seem like the task was doomed to fail. But the word of God came to the Prophet Habakkuk on the project.

> The Lord answered me and said, "Record the vision and inscribe it on tablets, that the one who reads it may run. For the vision is yet for the appointed time; it hastens toward the goal and it will not fail. Though it tarries, wait for it; for it will certainly come, it will not delay."
>
> Habakkuk 2:2,3 (NASB)

At 2 o'clock every morning, I was encouraged, exhilarated, and empowered by a clear vision of the race I was called to run and the opportunity to make some progress toward the finish line. I realized that "hard" and "easy" are relative terms. It was very clear to me who I was running for and why I was running. And that makes all the difference.

On Friday, September 4, Elle and I flew to General Santos City in Mindanao. Pastor Nowell Evangelista, Michael Chiongbian, and some of the staff members of Victory General Santos welcomed us. From there, we drove down to the tip of the southernmost province of the Philippines. We met with the mayor of Maasim and shared with him our vision for *RUN50*. He had seen the feature on a local news network and the story about Maasim being the starting point of the run and felt especially proud that his municipality was featured in primetime news. He was the first to partner with me for *RUN50* and give to the Real LIFE scholars.

After the meeting with the mayor, we headed to a resort where we stayed for the night (or at least part of the night) and prepared for Day 1. I tried to get some sleep while everyone else was busy with the preparations, but I was far too nervous and excited. At 11:00 p.m., I finally emerged from my room and was ready to go. That night, I had even received an encouraging text message from Joy Rojas, the only female to have completed a run across the Philippines. Michael Chiongbian, a businessman from Victory General Santos, and his driver transported Elle and me to the Maasim Municipal Hall. There was a small crowd of excited supporters waiting for us there—my pacers, Pinky Katipunan and Melinda Tongco; our videographers, Sharla Billena and Jeran Enrile; Pastor Nowell Evangelista with his staff, a few campus missionaries, and some Victory members; officers from the Philippine National Police; and local running enthusiasts who had joined us. It was like a fiesta. After meeting all of them, we filled a bottle with water from the ocean at the southernmost tip of the Philippines, then continued on to the *RUN50* starting point.

About 20 Real LIFE scholars surprised me by joining us for the last three kilometers of the first day's run. It was exhilarating beyond words to have these young people join me and cheer me on. They gave me the last ounce of energy I needed to finish on Day 1.

On Day 2, a Monday, after the run from General Santos to Malalag, Davao del Sur, my crew and I went back to General Santos because there were no hotels in Malalag. That night, Pastor Nowell and his wife Pinky, Michael, and the church staff surprised me with a birthday cake. The *RUN50* logo on the cake reminded me of how old I was and what I was attempting to do. The following day, after our run from Malalag to Santa Cruz, we met Pastor Alvin Supan of Victory Davao, his wife Vicky, some church staff members, and volunteers. They were waiting for me at the 50-km mark. After finishing Day 3, we drove to Davao City because there were also no hotels in Santa Cruz. We celebrated my 50th birthday for the second time.

PREACHING MY WAY TO APARRI

During my 44-day run, I visited mayors, politicians, and civil leaders across the Philippines. I took time to pray for each of them, and in some cases, preached the gospel. Many were believers and they more than welcomed it. But whether they liked it or not, this was my grand opportunity, and I was not inclined to bow my head for a moment of silent prayer. I prayed loudly and with great boldness for the cities, leaders, and nation as a whole.

I was reminded of how God spoke to Joshua. Upon the death of Moses, the Lord said to Joshua, "Moses my servant is dead. Now therefore arise, go over this Jordan, you and all this people, into the land that I am giving to them, to the people of Israel. Every place that the sole of your foot will tread upon I have given to you, just as I promised to Moses" (Joshua 1:2,3).

Well, I'm no Joshua, and this is not the Promised Land. I am, however, believing God for a great spiritual renewal across the Philippines. My team and I were running for Real LIFE scholars, but I was also running in faith, claiming every place I set my foot on for Christ's kingdom—that His kingdom would come to the

Philippines and that His will would be done here as it is in heaven. By my estimate, my feet touched the ground over 2,000,000 times. I was running across the nation to symbolically claim it for Christ as an act of faith. After all, "Faith is the assurance of things hoped for, the conviction of things not seen" (Hebrews 11:1).

The text of my sermon for most of the churches along the *RUN50* route was the same. I preached from Hebrews 12:1,2, about **running with endurance the race set before us.** If you perform the same task over and over, it's hard not to get better at it. That's also true with preaching. Hopefully, my sermon from Hebrews 12 got better as we worked our way northward across the Philippines. Repeating the same sermon can make it better to listen to but sometimes may seem boring for the preacher.

There are rock bands who are famous for their one great song— their one-hit wonder. They would only be invited to perform if they played that song; but because they perform it over and over, the band members may grow to hate it. This is not the case with preaching the Word of God. As I preached from Hebrews 12 again and again, it was like a never-ending vein of gold. The more I continue to dig into Hebrews 12 and its historical context, even after *RUN50*, the more amazing the things that continue to come out.

THE HEBREW SITUATION

Hebrews is one of my favorite books in the New Testament. No one knows for sure who wrote it, but the author is not as important as what he said. High on the list of the possible authors is the Apostle Paul because of the number of epistles he had written. But for several reasons, Bible scholars think it's unlikely that he was the author. They also say that while the epistles of the Apostle John were written on an elementary-school level and the rest of the New Testament was written for the common reader, the book of Hebrews in the original Greek reads like Shakespearean text. Though some have suggested that Paul could have asked a writer well trained in classical Greek to pen this book, it lacks the style of all the other Pauline epistles. The reference to Timothy in Hebrews 13:23 indicates that the author was in Paul's circle. Therefore, some scholars speculate that the epistle was written by Barnabas or Apollos, of whom it says in Acts 18:24 (NIV), "A Jew named Apollos, a native of Alexandria, came to Ephesus. He was a learned man, with a thorough knowledge of the Scriptures."

It seems that the epistle to the Hebrews was a homily (a sermon) that had been preached or taught frequently in the early church. The main theme of the epistle is easily recognizable: Christ is superior to the angels and to Moses. He is a better mediator and a better high priest in a better temple with a better sacrifice. He is the author of a better covenant with a better promise, Sabbath rest, and a better assurance. This is, in short, the essential message of the epistle to the Hebrews: Christ is far superior to the old covenant in every conceivable way.

The traditional Jewish community in the Roman Empire was shown some measure of toleration. They were neither favorites of the emperors, nor were they in danger of being thrown to the lions. Something else, however, was going on in the community of believers, an issue that the author was desperately trying to address. By the latter part of the first century, persecution was mounting against Christians who believed that Jesus rose from the dead after His crucifixion and that He alone would be the eternal judge of each and every person. When Christians in any corner of the Roman Empire contradicted the customary oath, "Caesar is Lord," with their own oath, "Jesus is Lord," it did not go well for them. That was as true in Jerusalem as it was in Rome. Apparently, there was in the church a group of Jews who had become Christians but in the face of persecution were separating themselves and flirting with the idea of retreating to Judaism from their most dangerous faith in Christ. This could be the context of the passage where the author challenged them to "consider how to stimulate one another to love and good deeds, not forsaking our own assembling together, as is the habit of some" (Hebrews 10:24,25, NASB).

As the author worked his way through all the aspects of Christ's superiority over the old covenant and its symbolic rituals, he inserted these digressions in which he issued his warning of falling back to Judaism. He does this in five sections that Wayne Grudem (1995, 134) has identified as "The Perils of the Hebrews." These digressions contain some of the strongest warnings and rebukes against Judaism found anywhere in the New Testament.

The Peril of Neglect (Hebrews 2:1-4)
... pay much closer attention to what we have heard, lest we drift away from it.... how shall we escape if we neglect such a great salvation? ...

Hebrews 2:1,3

The Peril of Unbelief (Hebrews 3:6-4:13)
Take care, brothers, lest there be in any of you an evil, unbelieving heart, leading you to fall away from the living God.

Hebrews 3:12

The Peril of Apostasy (Hebrews 6:4-6)
For it is impossible, in the case of those who have once been enlightened, who have tasted the heavenly gift, and have shared in the Holy Spirit ... and then have fallen away, to restore them again to repentance, since they are crucifying once again the Son of God to their own harm and holding him up to contempt.

Hebrews 6:4-6

The Peril of Judgment (Hebrews 10:26-31)
For if we go on sinning deliberately after receiving the knowledge of the truth, there no longer remains a sacrifice for sins, but a fearful expectation of judgment, and a fury of fire that will consume the adversaries.

Hebrews 10:26,27

The Peril of Refusal (Hebrews 12:25)
See that you do not refuse him who is speaking. For if they did not escape when they refused him who warned them on earth, much less will we escape if we reject him who warns from heaven.

Hebrews 12:25

The orderly discourse on the superiority of Christ, punctuated with these scathing rebukes and dire warnings, sends a clear message—God has done His perfect work in Christ—which put this smaller group of Jewish believers at a crossroad. If, after understanding the gospel and experiencing the transforming grace of God, they shrink back or turn away, they are then disqualified from the race, and all is lost.

The choice and consequences could not have been clearer.

The author of the epistle made his closing argument in Hebrews 11 and 12. Citing the faith, endurance, and perseverance of some of the Old Testament saints as well as the sufferings of Christ, he appeals to this group of Jews as to those who are running a great race.

All these saints ran by faith and suffered the painful consequences without even seeing or fully understanding the prize for which they were denying themselves. With an awareness of those onlookers from heaven, he urged them to pull themselves together, run with endurance, and finish well. Thus, my text for each *RUN50* sermon:

> Therefore, since we are surrounded by so great a cloud of witnesses, let us also lay aside every weight, and sin which clings so closely, and let us run with endurance the race that is set before us, looking to Jesus, the founder and perfecter of our faith, who for the joy that was set before him endured the cross, despising the shame, and is seated at the right hand of the throne of God. Consider him who endured from sinners such hostility against himself, so that you may not grow weary or fainthearted.
>
> Hebrews 12:1-3

RUN50 CHALLENGE

The epistle to the Hebrews makes the case for Christ with the most amazing clarity. It leaves no place for compromise and no middle ground. Throughout history, the church has enjoyed periods of peace and freedom, as well as seasons of intense persecution. And it is not far removed from our own experiences.

Individuals from Every Nation, our worldwide family of churches and ministries, have endured many threats and paid a high price to follow Christ. Their dedication and commitment is reminiscent of the great missionary and passionate disciple, William Borden.

A millionaire-turned-missionary, he died at the age of 25 in Egypt without reaching the Muslim community in China to whom he wanted to preach the gospel. On his gravestone is a saying attributed to him, from a series of notes written on the back of his Bible. This was written shortly before his death at the age of 25: "No reserves. No retreat. No regrets!"

How about you—are you running with endurance?

09
YOUR CALLING
THE RACE THAT IS SET BEFORE YOU

I wonder what sort of a tale we've fallen into?
J.R.R. TOLKIEN in The Lord of the Rings
Author

... let us also lay aside every weight, and sin which clings so closely, and let us run with endurance **the race that is set before us** *...*
HEBREWS 12:1

Ultramarathoners typically take some time off after long-distance runs, usually a few days to a few weeks, to allow their bodies to recuperate. The physical challenge of *RUN50* was not so much the 50-km runs but running them day after day, six days in a row, for seven weeks. It takes a different kind of mental and physical endurance.

You may recall that the *160-km Bataan Death March* in 2012 traced the entire journey of the Filipino and American prisoners of war who had surrendered to the Japanese. This race followed the same route as the *102-km Bataan Death March*, but it included the 53 km from Capas, Tarlac to Camp O'Donnell and the 5 km back to the Bataan Death March Kilometer Zero Memorial.

The last 58 km required a pacer. My first pacer was Alden, who ran 29 km with me beginning in San Fernando. Around the 112-km post, I became so tired that I couldn't keep my eyes open. They were already sore from lack of sleep. I've known of a lot of runners who quit because they were tired, but I'd never heard of a runner simply going to sleep while he was running. I began to think about how to make that work. Eventually, I asked Alden, "Bro, can I just close my eyes? If you can make sure the road is clear, I'll hold onto your shoulder."

"Sure, Pastor."

So we "run-walked" for a while. After a few km in light sleep holding onto Alden's shoulder, I was back to wide-awake running.

Alden handed me off to my second pacer, Jerome Bautista, at the halfway point, and we continued on toward Capas. Jerome is a very sharp and quick-witted banker and a member of Victory Pioneer. He's also good with a timely word of wisdom in the most desperate situations. Jerome was, therefore, the very pacer I needed in the final km of the longest race I had run to date.

By the 147-km post, I had been running for 25 hours. I was dizzy and had a hard time communicating or even thinking clearly. For about 13 km, I'd been battling with the idea of whether I would be able to finish this race or not. I was like a boxer swinging wildly against a far more superior opponent, being repeatedly knocked down and dared to quit. Even as the boxer struggles to get up and continue, the opponent lands a blow, and down he goes again. That scenario was repeated again and again.

I was not falling down but was definitely struggling to continue. The road from Mabalacat, Pampanga to Capas, Tarlac was a relentless opponent. The terrain had flattened out after a mountainous start. It had been a scorching hot day, with the sun relentlessly beating down on the runners. As we continued into the middle of the night, with every step I began to struggle with sharp pains in my feet. It felt like running on nails or sharp rocks. I was angry at my "opponent" and ready to quit.

As I struggled, I argued with Jerome, "Give me one reason I should finish this race." I must have asked him that question several times, but with the condition I was in, it's hard to remember. I'll never forget how Jerome finally replied.

"Pastor Ferdie, I understand that you're very tired and that you desperately want to quit. But I know someone personally who finished a much harder race in a much worse situation than you."

"Oh yeah?" I angrily replied. "Who is he?" I was expecting him to tell me a story of one of the most respected ultramarathoners in the world like Anton Krupicka, Dean Kamazes, Anna Frost, Scott Jurek, or the former Navy Seal, David Goggins.

"His name is Jesus Christ," Jerome said. "He suffered and died for your sins."

Oh man, I thought to myself. *That's what I'm supposed to say. This guy's preaching to the preacher!*

I don't remember if Jerome actually quoted the verse from the exhortation to the Hebrews, but I've thought about it many times since: "Consider him who endured from sinners such hostility against himself, so that you may not grow weary or fainthearted" (Hebrews 12:3). That verse was the culmination of the exhortation that began in chapter 11—an appeal to all the examples of men and women of faith who endured and persevered despite great pain and suffering. In addition to these examples recorded ages ago, I was living with my very own inspiration—my son, Philip. Remembering those who have finished their races, as well as those running with me every day, has helped me keep my life and my little struggles in perspective. With reference to the great sufferings of those who have gone before, a friend of mine occasionally says, "This is a trial, not a tragedy. Far worse things have happened to far greater people."

Approaching the last one and a half km of the race, Jerome said, "You know what? I think I'm going to cry when you finish this race."

"What? Why are you going to cry? I'm the one who is struggling to finish."

"Because I've come to realize," he said, "that this is your destiny. God has called you to do this. There are many younger, stronger, faster runners who are far more qualified to do this. But here you are."

Jerome was a great encouragement, and his words were also prophetic—as the most encouraging words often are. In 2011, we had run the *102-km Bataan Death March* to raise money for Real LIFE scholars. There were, however, no sponsors or pledges for this 160-km race, and a run across the Philippines had not yet entered our minds. But God was indeed calling me to run an even greater race for an even greater prize. I just didn't know yet what it was.

The significance of those final 13 km occurred to me years later. I had been quite burnt out after completing that race. If Jerome had not been there and if I had quit that race with such a short distance remaining, would I have even been open to the idea of *RUN50*, the project that three years later produced such a grand prize for the Real LIFE scholars? That's the importance of persevering—to finish what you've started. It establishes a foundation of faith as a stepping stone when faced with an even greater challenge. It's like David's response to Goliath: "Your servant has struck down both lions and bears, and this uncircumcised Philistine shall be like one of them" (1 Samuel 17:36).

BECAUSE IT'S YOUR DESTINY

The race you're running is not the result of your own seeking or choosing. Jesus said to His disciples, "You did not choose me, but I chose you and appointed you that you should go and bear fruit" (John 15:16).

Appointed who?

Appointed **you**!

In J.R.R. Tolkien's epic, *The Lord of the Rings*, Samwise Gamgee describes for Frodo Baggins the nature of the adventure they'd begun:

> "The brave things in the old tales and songs, Mr. Frodo—adventures, as I used to call them. I used to think that they were things the wonderful folk of the stories went out and looked for, because they wanted them, because they were exciting and life was a bit dull, a kind of a sport, as you might say.

"But that's not the way of it with the tales that really mattered, or the ones that stay in the mind. Folks seem to have been just landed in them, usually—their paths were laid that way, as you put it."

You didn't seek God; He sought you. You didn't find Jesus; He found you. In other words, it was by God's initiative that the course of your race is "laid that way." There may be people more qualified in many ways, but God is the author of the race He has called you to run.

CALLING AS STEWARDSHIP

Paul understood that his calling as the apostle to the Gentiles was not something he chose but something that was laid upon him. He consistently referred to his calling as a stewardship entrusted to him.

> To the church in Galatia: "They saw that I had been **entrusted with the gospel** to the uncircumcised, just as Peter had been **entrusted with the gospel** to the circumcised."
>
> Galatians 2:7

> To the church in Corinth: "This is how one should regard us, as servants of Christ and **stewards of the mysteries of God.**"
>
> 1 Corinthians 4:1

He also understood that God's plan was not just for him but for a world full of Gentiles. In other words, he saw his calling not in terms of who he was (his position), but in terms of Whom he was called to serve.

> To the church in Ephesus: "For this reason I, Paul, a prisoner of Christ Jesus **on behalf of you Gentiles**—assuming that you have heard of the **stewardship of God's grace** that was **given to me for you** . . ."
>
> Ephesians 3:1,2

> To the church in Colossae: "I became a minister according to the stewardship from God that was **given to me for you**,

to make the word of God fully known, the mystery hidden
for ages and generations but now revealed to his saints."
Colossians 1:25,26

The Apostle Paul in no way saw his monumental efforts as anything more than the obligation his stewardship demanded. Think of it this way: if the goal of running is to receive a reward, we can freely choose to run for it or not. It all depends on how much you value that reward. We can choose to run for the prize or become spectators. Not surprisingly, the Apostle Paul didn't see it that way. The stewardship entrusted to him gave him no such choice:

> Again to the church in Corinth: "For if I preach the gospel, that gives me no ground for boasting. For **necessity is laid upon me**. Woe to me if I do not preach the gospel! For if I do this of my own will, I have a reward, but if not of my own will, **I am still entrusted with a stewardship**."
> 1 Corinthians 9:16,17

According to him, he should not be alone in this stewardship mentality. Second- and third-generation leaders should have that same perspective.

> To his co-laborer, Titus: "For the overseer, as God's steward, must be above reproach . . ."
> Titus 1:7

> To his son in the Lord: "O Timothy, guard what has been entrusted to you . . ."
> 1 Timothy 6:20 (NASB)

And finally, the Apostle Peter also understood his calling and the calling of each person in the church in terms of their stewardship of what was given to them. Not everyone has the same gifting or is called to run the same race.

> To the churches in Asia Minor, Peter wrote: "As each has received a gift, use it to serve one another, as **good stewards of God's varied grace:** whoever speaks, as one who speaks oracles of God; whoever serves, as one who serves by the

strength that God supplies—in order that in everything God may be glorified through Jesus Christ."

1 Peter 4:10,11

RUN WITH ENDURANCE

Does the way you think about your particular calling make a difference? Do you see it as a path you have chosen or a race that God has set before you? Is it something that you want to do for God or a stewardship (responsibility) entrusted to you? Is it just promotion to a higher position or a calling to be a servant? How are you running your race, and does it really make a difference?

It absolutely makes a difference. A **big** difference.

Back in the 1980s, I read an article in a little publication called *Table Talk*, written by Walter Walker, the campus pastor of Steve, Rice, and several other leaders who came from Mississippi State University. I still have some of the old issues, including one on being "Entrusted with the Gospel," where he commented on endurance and the way we understand our calling.

Ministry leaders have been known to boldly challenge their listeners or members to "get a vision to do something for God" or some variation of that. The contrasting perspectives look like this:

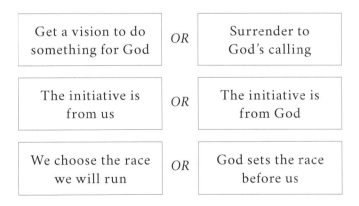

In our desire to do something for God, it's easy to think of our passionate, dedicated years of service as doing God a favor rather than being indebted to God as the One who entrusted us with the responsibility of stewardship.

| My service is doing God a favor | OR | My service is surrendering to His will |

| My service as a favor makes me God's creditor | OR | My service as a steward makes me His debtor |

Favors are optional; debts are obligatory. When it comes to endurance, resilience, and perseverance in the race laid out before us, it's much easier to stop doing favors than it is to stop paying your debts.

I can hear some of you thinking now, *Obligation, prisoner, woe is me if I don't . . . that's pretty heavy. What about our freedom in Christ? What about the yoke being easy and the burden light?* I understand that people can struggle under a false religious burden. However, that burden is most often based on individuals striving to please God and never feeling that they have done enough. The good news is that Christ has done everything that can be done to secure our right standing with God. Freedom in Christ is understanding that there's nothing we can do to add to what He has already done. In other words, we don't have to conjure up a list of things to do to feel that we are in right standing with Him or to please Him. Saying yes to the race He has set before us is a response to God's grace given to us in Christ, not a contribution to it.

ADVANCE STEWARDSHIP

Endurance in my little run across the Philippines was a realization about who I was running for (the Real LIFE scholars and Philip) and why I was running (because I felt God's call to do it). I had been entrusted with a stewardship on behalf of those I was called to serve.

In the earlier chapters, I talked about becoming a champion—that is, championing the cause of those in need just as Jesus Christ became our "Savior and Champion" (Isaiah 19:20, NASB). There seem to be several levels of championship:

1. Running to raise money for those in need, which unbelievers do as much as Christians

2. Identifying so deeply with those you are called to serve that your championship becomes a passion (my son, Philip)
3. Understanding our stewardship in terms of championship; in the words of the Apostle Paul, "I became a minister according to the stewardship from God that was **given to me for you**" (Colossians 1:25)

RUN50 CHALLENGE

In *The Lord of the Rings*, the conversation between Samwise Gamgee and Frodo Baggins continued:

> "But I expect they had lots of chances, like us, of turning back, only they didn't. And if they had, we shouldn't know, because they'd have been forgotten. We hear about those who just went on—and not all to a good end, mind you; at least not to what folk inside a story and not outside it call a good end.
>
> "But those aren't always the best tales to hear, though they may be the best tales to get landed in!
>
> "I wonder what sort of a tale we've fallen into?"

If I am the initiator of my calling to serve God, in the face of intense difficulties, I might simply choose an easier and more convenient vision. The author of the epistle to the Hebrews addressed that temptation and crisis of their faith. In the face of persecution, they were tempted to shrink back to a safer and more convenient confession of faith. That was, in fact, the sin which was clinging so closely to them (Hebrews 12:1).

Are you trying to dream up a big vision for your life? Are you striving to bolster your assurance by contributing to what Christ has already done? You need to stop your striving and accept the fact that your service to God is a response to grace, **not** a contribution to it.

That being said, your dreams and your vision could be, and probably are, far too small. God sees you with eyes of faith—what you could do and be with the power of the Holy Spirit. Remember, surrendering to God's calling will accomplish more for Christ's kingdom than all the dreams and visions we can conjure up on our own.

So, have you surrendered to run the race He has set before you?

10
YOUR FOCUS
FIXING YOUR EYES ON JESUS

Experience has taught me how important it is to just keep going, focusing on running fast and relaxed. Eventually pain passes and the flow returns. It's part of racing.

FRANK SHORTER
1972 *Munich Olympics*, Gold Medalist, Marathon

. . . let us run with endurance the race that is set before us, ***fixing our eyes*** *on Jesus . . .*

HEBREWS 12:1,2 (NASB)

In the epistle to the Hebrews, the anonymous author targeted a specific audience—and targeted they were indeed. Like a laser-guided sniper rifle, he aimed his exhortation at a particular group within the church that was on the verge of returning to the sacrificial traditions of the old covenant. They probably didn't see it as backsliding but merely adopting a more convenient form of Christianity—"Christianity Lite," you might say. Or perhaps they were aiming for "synchronicity," a less controversial blend of Christianity and Judaism. The writer of the epistle to the Hebrews made a compelling case for the supremacy of Christ and aimed his warnings at those who were contemplating a retreat from that confession. A retreat would mean an abandonment of the faith altogether. The truth is, since God has already done His ultimate work in Christ, there is no going back to the old covenant.

Perhaps these individuals who were teetering on the edge of apostasy sat around in their small group talking about Moses, about the temple, and about the way their ancestors had worshipped for thousands of years.

They may have asked, "Is this new faith in Jesus Christ worth the enormous difficulties that come with it?"

The warning and exhortation in the epistle to the Hebrews was: "Just stop it! Stop longing for the old covenant. Stop looking for a compromise. 'Run with endurance the race that is set before you, fixing your eyes on Jesus.' He is the better high priest, He is the better mediator, and He made the better sacrifice."

UP AND DOWN

There were a lot of arduous ascents and perilous descents during *RUN50*. If runners don't know how to manage their energy, they can become completely exhausted climbing a big hill. It was like that in many places but none more extreme than the road from San Ricardo to Libagon—the first 50 km of our run through Southern Leyte on Day 12. What an amazing route! It seemed to me at the time to be the most beautiful place in the world. But it was up and down, up and down, and so very tiring. Talk about steep! I didn't have a level to actually measure the incline, but my civil-engineering senses estimated that in some places the grade had to be almost 45 degrees. It was a cross between running and mountain climbing. It took 12 hours and 35 minutes to finish that day's run.

When attacking steep hills or difficult terrain, I've adopted the habit of fixing my eyes on a spot in the road about 10 m in front of me. I don't look at the hilltop and don't look around at the scenery, just my position plus 10. Going into my 10-m focus is, for me, like mentally shifting to low gear. I'm not thinking about the 2,180 km of *RUN50* or (in the case of the *160-km Bataan Death March*) the remaining 13 km when Jerome talked me through the finish. I'm just fixing my eyes on the next 10 m and shutting out everything else.

The Greek word *aphorōntes*, translated as "fixing our eyes" in the New American Standard Version or "looking to" in the English Standard Version, can also be translated as "looking away." Consequently, the Amplified Version says, "looking away from all that will distract us and focusing our eyes on Jesus."

The author of the epistle gave a written prescription for the extremely difficult position in which the church found itself. He told them to not only fix their attention on Jesus, but to "look away" from all things that were threatening their faith. That is to say, they needed to guard their hearts from doubts and fears by focusing intently on the person and work of Jesus Christ.

In happy times, when we are living in abundance, it's easy to have big dreams and strong faith. In such times, our personal and ministry visions all seem possible, if not inevitable. When dark days come upon us, however, we begin to question and wonder about those dreams. A multitude of other concerns and questions that are hard—if not impossible—to answer begin to assault our minds, as if they've been waiting in reserve for just the right moment to flood onto the battlefield. A barrage of questions begin to emerge: *What if this happens? What if that doesn't work out? What about that?* Discipline yourselves, the writer says, to focus intently on Christ. Shut out everything else you can.

A friend of mine in the ministry told me about going through an extended period of deep darkness and disillusionment. He battled with a lot of doubts, couldn't imagine any way that all things would work for his good, and became quite depressed about his life and future. He was starting down the road to cynicism. Struggling to hang onto his faith and vision, daily prayer walks turned into a slow and deliberate recitation of the Apostles' Creed. He would begin, "I believe in God, the Father Almighty."

Yep, I believe that, he would say to himself.

"Creator of heaven and earth."

Yep, believe that too.

"And in Jesus Christ, His only Son, our Lord."

And so he went on through the rest of the creed.

Yes ... Yes ... Yes ...

At the end, he would typically pray, "Lord, I believe all of that, but beyond those things, I have no idea. I don't know if everything or anything is going to turn out for good. I don't even know if it's really supposed to. I don't know if there's a plan, if there's a future for me, or if You're done with me. All I know is ... I believe in God, the Father Almighty, Creator of heaven and earth ..."

And he'd repeat the process every day until the end of his walk and, in time, after many such prayer walks, he made it over the hump. He later shared his experience and what he learned from it:

> It seems that we allow a lot of presumptions and expectations to grow up on top of our fundamental beliefs about God. My troubles were relatively insignificant when compared to the fiery trials other people face. It was just that things weren't lining up with my *vision for my perfect world*. I think a lot of our trials and troubles are not attacks on our fundamental beliefs but upon our presumptions and expectations. Through the whole experience, it seemed the Holy Spirit was pruning off all my overgrown presumptions in order to get me back to focusing on simply what God has done for me in Christ.

The exhortation given to the Hebrews would benefit any person who has ever walked through darkness, doubt, or discouragement: "Run with endurance the race that is set before you. Guard your hearts and mind against the distractions (and presumptions) that are warring against your faith. Focus your attention singularly on what God has done in Jesus Christ."

Fixing our eyes on Jesus is, for me, a lot like fixing my eyes 10 m ahead during a difficult climb. Whenever I feel the need to get into that focus, I am reminded of the words of Elisabeth Elliot (1992). Her husband was Jim Elliot, a missionary who was attacked and killed by the Auca Indians. While waiting for news of her husband before learning of his death, she said, "When you don't know what to do next, just do the thing in front of you."

RUNNING STEEP HILLS

When climbing steep inclines, experienced runners use small steps, swinging both arms up to the chin. The swinging motion gives you an added push going up the hill. You have to force yourself to be patient. Focus on your form and on the next 10 m.

Descending a steep incline requires a different technique and even more intense focus.

Bend your knees slightly, take small "rolling steps," lower your hands to your side, and shorten your stride again. Running down long inclines creates additional pounding on your knees, which can quickly turn into soreness and eventually into injury. Again, you have to be patient and resist the temptation to use the downward slope to make up the time with big strides. If your wobbly legs can't keep up with your forward momentum, it's hard to slow down. At that point, you're in real danger of losing control and seriously injuring yourself. On steep inclines, whether you're ascending or descending, you have to focus and be extra careful with every step.

Whether running a race, a business, or a church, leaders can easily become careless when they feel like there is so much momentum behind them. They can lose focus and stumble, sometimes in subtle but significant ways. We had a rude awakening to that possibility in September 2009.

We were all still feeling the excitement from the 25th anniversary celebration of Victory at the Araneta Coliseum, which had been the venue for two consecutive convergences on July 24, 2009. We were riding a great wave of momentum, and all things seemed possible. Two dozen key leaders from Victory in Metro Manila were working on a strategic plan for future growth. Someone wrote a very big number on the board that represented our attendance goal for the next decade. Everyone took a deep breath and, with a growing sense of excitement, began to focus on the goal of more than doubling our current attendance.

Pastor Steve, who was the president of Every Nation by then, was in that meeting. Though Pastor Steve was now President Steve, he hadn't changed his habit of equipping and empowering others to lead. He came determined, as usual, not to interfere but to let the Filipino team he had developed take the lead. However, he knew something was wrong, even though he couldn't put his finger on it.

He later explained, "As we examined our numbers, all of which seemed to be growing, my eyes fell on one set of numbers that had flatlined over the last four years (and was even showing hints of decline)."

While church attendance was exploding, the number of Victory groups and the number of Victory group leaders were not. As our strategic planning group began to evaluate things more closely, we began to see leadership voids everywhere. The result was a radical renewal of our emphasis on Victory groups and developing Victory group leaders. We had gotten distracted by the momentum of our growth and had begun fixing our eyes on the growing church attendance, rather than making disciples and training leaders. In terms of the race that had been set before us at Victory, we were running down a steep incline, gaining momentum, beginning to lose control, and forgetting to fix our focus on what Jesus had called us to do—make disciples.

RUN50 CHALLENGE

The goal of life is to honor God in the way you run the race set before you. It's not about how fast you run or how far you get before you finish. The manner in which you run makes all the difference. Sadly, lots of great leaders have stumbled on a downhill run. We can only honor God in our race by fixing our attention on the person and work of Christ alone—not on our positions, acclaim, financial resources, abilities, ministry success, or the lack thereof. All of those things are merely distractions that divert our focus onto lesser things and away from what honors God.

The temptation to lose focus is greatest when things are either very difficult or very easy; when you're wildly successful or failing miserably; when you're climbing an impossibly steep hill or running out of control down the side of a mountain. In any case, fix your focus intently on Jesus, looking away from the sin that can so easily entangle and trip you up. Lots of great leaders have stumbled on a downhill run.

Are you looking away from the sin that can so easily entangle and trip you up, and fixing your eyes intently on Jesus?

11
YOUR VISION
KEEPING PACE WITH AN EXPANDING STEWARDSHIP

We all have dreams. But in order to make dreams come into reality, it takes an awful lot of determination, dedication, self-discipline, and effort.

JESSE OWENS
1936 Berlin Olympics, four-time Gold Medalist

*... who for the **joy set before Him** endured the cross ...*

HEBREWS 12:2 (NASB)

Clarity is a wonderful thing. In *Alice's Adventures in Wonderland* by Lewis Carroll (1998, 89), there's an often-quoted conversation between Alice and the Cheshire Cat:

> Alice: "Would you tell me, please, which way I ought to go from here?"
>
> The Cheshire Cat: "That depends a good deal on where you want to get to."
>
> Alice: "I don't much care where."
>
> The Cheshire Cat: "Then it doesn't much matter which way you go."
>
> Alice: "... So long as I get somewhere."
>
> The Cheshire Cat: "Oh, you're sure to do that, if only you walk long enough."

Alice was unclear about where she wanted to go, and the Cheshire Cat's suggestion only compounded her dilemma. Often, obedience is not the most difficult thing with which we have to contend.

It's the lack of clarity (the lack of a clear vision forward) that just sucks the energy right out of you. People, at some of the most frustrating times in their lives, say to themselves, *If I just knew what to do, I'd do it.* Such an unclear vision sucks the energy right out of you.

We talk a lot about empowering as one of the key aspects of our discipleship journey in Victory. Very early on as a Christian, long before the formulation of that journey, I learned what having a clear vision could be like. To be more precise, I felt empowered by the vision others instilled in and entrusted to me.

IMPARTING VISION

In the early days of Victory in U-Belt, Pastor Steve heard about a large church movement in Manila—the Jesus is Lord Church led by Bro. Eddie Villanueva. At that time, they were meeting in an open-air quadrangle at Araullo High School on the corner of Taft and United Nations Avenue. Pastor Steve decided to visit and observe, but he didn't go alone. In fact, he rarely did things alone. On this occasion, I was privileged to accompany him.

That was my first exposure to a church movement outside the small band of students in the Tandem Cinema basement. This outdoor church had no chairs, and therefore, no aisles. Their ushers collected the offering by wandering aimlessly through the crowd with baskets. As an usher in our church, this seemed unorganized and chaotic to me. My "usher-pride" was kicking in.

They were passionately worshipping God together, standing throughout the entire worship service. In the middle of the long-standing meeting, Pastor Steve leaned over and whispered to me, "Ferdie, I want you to dream . . . Someday, we will grow so large that we won't have a place to meet."

It had never occurred to me before that there could be anything bigger or better than what was going on in the basement of Tandem Cinema. However, that night, standing in the middle of that quadrangle, I began to see a bigger picture. Did I see Victory as it exists today? Hardly. I didn't have the faith for that kind of thinking. But my vision has continued to expand as I've struggled to keep pace with the challenges of exponential growth.

EMPOWERED BY THE VISION

Not long after our visit to the big outdoor church, I was in a leadership training class being taught by Pastor Steve. It's pretty funny to think about it now. We had all just barely dried off from the waters of baptism, and yet we were being trained as leaders of a fledgling church. Pastor Steve was older than most of us by just a few years and had only a year's experience as a campus missionary at Mississippi State University where he had led a small group of students. In the eyes of church-planting experts, Steve and Deborah would not have been considered even close to ready. That was, in fact, the concern of the group that had sponsored the team of American student missionaries in 1984. "Who is this Steve Murrell," they asked, "and what has he ever done?" Nonetheless, we considered ourselves highly privileged that Steve and Deborah had stayed to lead the church.

Pastor Steve's first assignment to us during that class was: "Write down your 10-year vision for our church."

Ten years? I thought.

I was on fire for Christ and living in the moment. Ten years seemed like a lifetime to a 20-year-old college student. Nevertheless, I did my best to come up with a vision.

I don't remember if Pastor Steve said it then, but it occurs to me now that Jesus gave the same assignment to His young disciples. "Do you not say, 'There are yet four months, then comes the harvest'? Look, I tell you, lift up your eyes, and see that the fields are white for harvest" (John 4:35). He seemed to be saying, "Don't think this is going to take a long time. Begin to see the harvest by faith, even though it seems to be a long way off."

This was the vision I wrote down: "I would speak to the entire nation for at least 30 minutes and present the gospel to every Filipino." After first envisioning *RUN50*, I spent three years training and contemplating that run across the Philippines. As I worked my way northward on the Philippine National Highway and preached the gospel to 21 mayors and government officials, I remembered what I had written 30 years earlier.

As the memory came back to me, I shouted, "Yes! From one end to the other, preaching the gospel." Sure, I know that the entire nation had not gathered together to hear me preach, it hadn't happened in 10 years, and not every Filipino heard what I had to say (though a great number had heard about *RUN50*). Nonetheless, recalling that vision gave me a big shot of spiritual adrenalin. What's even better is that the eventual fulfillment is something we will all accomplish together. The Lord replied to Habakkuk's inquiries: "Record the vision and inscribe it on tablets, that the one who reads it may run. For the vision is yet for the appointed time; it hastens toward the goal and it will not fail. Though it tarries, wait for it; for it will certainly come, it will not delay" (Habakkuk 2:2,3, NASB).

STARGAZING FOR VICTORY

In 2001, I was serving as one of the lead pastors of Victory Ortigas with Pastor Steve. Judy was heading Kids' Church, Paolo Punzalan was the Kids' Church pastor, and Rico Ricafort was the youth pastor. We gathered a group of about 120 teenagers from Victory Makati and Victory Ortigas, many of them new believers, for a two-day camp at Caliraya Recreation Center. Paolo, Rico, Judy, and I taught the sessions.

On the first night, we had a one-on-one session with each of them. Many were carrying heavy baggage from their past. We prayed with each of them to be released from spiritual bondage—from the "sin which clings so closely" (Hebrews 12:1).

The next day, we explained from the Scriptures who they are in Christ having received salvation by grace through faith. They had been freed from the powers that had enslaved them and were beginning to realize their righteousness in Christ. They were growing in faith right before our eyes. Then we taught them about the Holy Spirit, and most (if not all) had spiritual encounters and were filled with the Spirit.

At the close of the weekend retreat, I decided to bring them out to an open field. Since we were 80 km outside Manila, the night was clear and the stars had never been brighter. I asked them to lie down, look up to the heavens, and try to estimate how many stars they could see from one horizon to another. It was an impossible task. No one could count them.

God had done the same thing with Abram. "And behold, the word of the Lord came to him . . . And he brought him outside and said, 'Look toward heaven, and number the stars, if you are able to number them.' Then he said to him, 'So shall your offspring be.' And he believed the Lord, and he counted it to him as righteousness" (Genesis 15:4-6). God was trying to expand Abram's vision concerning the promises being made to him so that he would not limit what God wanted to do through him by his lack of faith.

He was building Abram's faith.

After a few minutes, I told the group of teenagers to stand. "You cannot count the stars," I said, "but I want you to dream, and dream big. I want you to have a vision of God's future and His plan for you. I want you to see yourself making an impact in your generation for Christ with His power. I want you to begin seeing yourselves as leaders of multitudes."

Many of those visionary teenagers are now leaders in Victory. These include Joseph Bonifacio (director of Every Nation Campus in the Philippines), Patrick Mercado (a lead pastor in Victory Fort), Dan Monterde (a missionary to Australia), King Lucero (a pastor in Victory Alabang), Varsha Daswani (who serves in the Communications and Technology Department of Every Nation Philippines), and Janelle Odero (who serves Victory in Metro Manila).

That was the first *Victory Weekend* for the youth. Since then, we've had hundreds more.

KEEPING THE PACE

Like the author of the epistle to the Hebrews, I have a specific audience in mind when I preach, but it isn't those contemplating apostasy. It's more likely to be those who have been fully committed to their race and have, in fact, been running very well. However, the particular course that has been laid out for them is quite long and getting steeper. The challenge for them is to keep pace with their own sense of calling and vision.

That's something I'm learning as well. The stewardship entrusted to me today has greatly expanded. Sometimes I feel like it has expanded more than I could have imagined. However, if my vision does not keep pace with our expanding vision for Victory, I would fall behind, struggle to catch up, and possibly stumble along the way. As a straggler, I would be at risk of losing my way or simply dropping out.

Through the years Pastor Steve has continued to be my mentor and a source of inspiration. He's a great example of what it means to keep pace with an expanding vision. In the early days of discipleship training, there was a lot of instruction and correction—do this, don't do that; do it this way, not that way.

Over 30 years have gone by since that first leadership training class, and today, I feel more personally challenged by Pastor Steve than ever. But it's almost never in the form of personal instruction or correction. His lifestyle, marriage, parenting, spiritual disciplines, leadership philosophy, and forward thinking serve as ever-present challenges to me.

Pastor Steve doesn't just stay on pace; he always seems to be setting the pace. He was pressing the issue of a tangible and reproducible discipleship process in the mid-1980s at Victory, when some churches were only giving lip service to discipleship. When most others were satisfied with the status quo, he had the vision for Every Nation Music and for the Every Nation Theological Seminary, to provide advanced training for our pastors. Though we were just a bunch of students at the beginning, Pastor Steve repeatedly inspired us to envision a day when we would be making disciples of those from all walks of life—from the government, business sector, academe, and entertainment industry.

Pastor Steve has a remarkable ability to serve Every Nation as both a grinder and visionary. His high commitment to daily spiritual disciplines makes him like an ultramarathoner who knows how to tackle a challenging hill by fixing his eyes on the next few steps of the race—the 10-m-forward focus. At the same time, I think he has been entrusted with a keen sense of stewardship, a responsibility that has continued to grow exponentially. The more our movement grows, the farther ahead he projects his focus. One of his recent books has a title that matches his perspective—*100 Years from Now*. He's most likely to envision all the dynamics of a big race—like a 2,180-km run across the Philippines or for Every Nation to have a campus ministry and church in every nation. While others in Every Nation may be celebrating their success, he's most likely to be focused on those we are not yet reaching.

Pastor Steve is a great example, but he's not the only one. I've had the privilege of walking and working with many others who have had a great impact on me: Dr. Jun Escosar, Bishop Manny Carlos, Pastor Joey Bonifacio, and Bishop Juray Mora to name a few. I am also humbled to lead hundreds of other Victory pastors in Metro Manila.

These men exemplify what it means for us to keep pace with an expanding stewardship that has been entrusted to us. As a young disciple and even as a rookie campus missionary, my race was pretty simple and on repeat: preach the gospel, make disciples, train leaders. Life was good.

Life is still good. I'm still preaching the gospel, making disciples, and training leaders. As a consequence of the growing stewardship entrusted to me, I'm greatly challenged to pick up the pace. I have to study, pray, counsel, serve, and think ahead on a more intense level.

RUN50 CHALLENGE

To repeat a point made in an earlier chapter, leadership is not about a position or title. It's about taking on a greater level of service and responsibility. The Apostle Paul wrote to Timothy, "If anyone aspires to the office of overseer, he desires a noble task" (1 Timothy 3:1). However, you cannot run at the pace of those who straggle behind or even with those who run with the main pack. If they expect others to follow, leaders have to lead the way by example.

Some of Pastor Steve's words from 1984 about staying ahead and growing in my faith remain with me until today: "As long as you stay one chapter ahead, you can disciple that new believer. But if he passes you, then he'll disciple you." Though leadership development is much more complex than simply staying one chapter ahead, the point remains. As the vision for our race expands, the challenge for all current and future Victory group leaders, including myself, remains: are we keeping pace with the expanding stewardship entrusted to each of us?

12
YOUR FAITH
LEARNING FROM YOUR HEROES

Crossing the starting line may be an act of courage, but crossing the finish line is an act of faith. Faith is what keeps us going when nothing else will. Faith is the emotion that will give you victory over your past, the demons in your soul, and all of those voices that tell you what you can and cannot do—what you can and cannot be.

JOHN "THE PENGUIN" BINGHAM
Marathon Runner

*. . . let us run with endurance the race that is set before us, fixing our eyes on Jesus, the **author and perfecter of faith** . . .*

HEBREWS 12:1,2 (NASB)

Recovering from the arduous *160-km Bataan Death March* in 2012 had been a slow process, both physically and emotionally. Three months had gone by since that race, and I was still in pain and burnt out from running. I had all but concluded that I was done as an ultramarathoner. However, my newfound vision to run across the Philippines and raise funds for Real LIFE scholars inspired me to keep going.

At that point, I hadn't figured out how I was going to manage a transnational run across the Philippines. The *160-km Bataan Death March* had taken me 28:44:46, and I had barely made it to the finish line. The Philippine islands stretch out over 2,000 km from one end to another. So, to run the entire length of the Philippines would take me . . . Well, I hadn't figured that out yet or a hundred other details, for that matter. How much would I run each day and for how many days? How long would it take to train for such a run? Could I get pacers to volunteer for such an endeavor? Could I take time off from my responsibilities at work? Even if these and many other questions remained unanswered, I simply locked in on the vision.

Many years ago, I heard an American missionary talking about a significant challenge he felt called to undertake. The point of his story and message was that, although you can dream about doing great things, investigate all options, develop strategies, calculate risks, and make temporary plans, they all circle around the real issue—your willingness to step out in faith. He talked about people who avoided taking that step for as long as they could with statements like: "If the Lord provides . . . If the Lord opens the door . . . If I still feel led when the time comes . . . If so-and-so agrees . . . If it all works out . . ."

Most of those are just "equivocations." I had to look up the definition of that word in the *Oxford Dictionaries* website to make sure I was using it properly.

> **e·quiv·o·ca·tion:** *the use of ambiguous language to conceal the truth or to avoid committing oneself*

Yes, that's exactly what I meant to say. However, it's not that I've always been the high standard of decisiveness. There have been times when I was like a frightened pilot circling the field trying to summon the courage to land. On the day the Holy Spirit was convicting me to repent and receive Christ's gift of salvation, I sat there clinging to my seat, terrified of what others might think. As time went by and my faith grew, I've tried to boldly and decisively respond to the leading of the Holy Spirit.

The American missionary taught me that faith only begins when you lock into what you believe God has called you to do. So after reading Father Picx's blog, I locked in on the vision for what came to be known as *RUN50*. From that point onward, it was not a matter of **if** but **how** I would finish the race.

HEROES OF FAITH

The author of the epistle to the Hebrews exhorts his wavering readers to consider the example of those who by faith accomplished extraordinary things against overwhelming odds. The story of Caleb, the son of Jephunneh and the servant of Moses, is one of those I've spent a lot of time considering. He has almost become my faith coach, speaking to me from the pages of Scripture.

It's a familiar story and great example of locking in on your calling with a **not-if-but-how** commitment. The children of Israel on their way from Egypt to the Promised Land camped in the wilderness of Paran. There, God spoke to Moses, instructing him to send one man from each tribe of Israel, twelve in all, as spies to Canaan. These men spent 40 days spying out the land. They came back with reports of extraordinary fruitfulness but even stronger enemies. Ten of those who saw the Promised Land were smitten with fear and gave a bad report. The King James Version calls it an "evil report" (Numbers 13:32). Only Joshua and Caleb had the faith to enter the Promised Land. Caleb said, "Let us go up at once and occupy it, for we are well able to overcome it" (Numbers 13:30).

The evil report of the 10 spread like wildfire throughout the camp. Consequently, the Israelites *en masse* gave up hope of entering the Promised Land and instead longed to go back to their slave-masters in Egypt. God showed His displeasure over their readiness to quit and declared that they would wander in the wilderness for 40 years—one year for every day they had spent spying out the land.

Isn't it amazing how people can view the same risks and rewards and come back with completely opposite recommendations? The assessment of Joshua and Caleb represents a perspective founded on God's promise. The perspective of the 10 other spies was quite different. In fact, they had lost sight of their mission. Moses had sent them to figure out **how** to take the land—not **if** they could.

Apparently, they had never personally locked in on God's promise and calling.

Below are just a few lessons from this story for Victory group leaders.

1. Fear and doubt are contagious; so is quitting. During the first week of *RUN50*, my left ankle began to swell. For a couple of days, I put ice on it and kept it elevated after each day's run. I kept saying, "It's no big deal. I'll get better as I go." However, the constant pounding of my feet on the road made it worse. We were six days into a 44-day run, and thousands of friends, church members, runners, and well-wishers were following our progress. More and more people were making pledges through the website. Advance teams were setting up meetings with government officials along the way. Everyone was excited. On the road, crew members periodically massaged my foot and ankle as I tried to remain positive, block out the pain, and stay focused on the day's run—employing my 10-m-forward focus. Some people from the *barrio* came out to see what was going on. When they looked at my ankle, they didn't say what they were thinking, but I could see it in their faces: *What's happening to the Running Pastor? Can he really run all the way to Aparri on that ankle?*

All they actually said was "good luck," but I could feel their reservations about my ability to go much farther. I think what they really wanted to say was: "Good luck, because you're really going to need it."

I wouldn't call it an "evil report." They were just responding to what they could see with their own eyes. In the story, the 10 spies who gave the "evil report" caused fear and doubt to spread like wildfire among the rest of the Israelites because they depended only on what they could see. Seeing the look on the spectators' faces made me realize how contagious fear and doubt could be, and how quickly a discouraging report can cause things to fall apart. But the onlookers had underestimated my resolve or the degree to which I had locked in on the vision to finish my race for the Real LIFE scholars. At the end of Day 6, I called Dr. Jojo Rivera and asked him a few questions about my ankle, but I never really told him how bad it looked. And I never told anyone else until *RUN50* was over.

Eventually, the swelling subsided, and I made it all the way to the northern tip of the Philippines. Without the years of training, without the experience of enduring the pain, and without faith in the One who sustained me, I could have become overwhelmed by doubts and fears and ended up quitting.

2. Your self-image can hinder your faith. Jesus said to His disciples, "Let the greatest among you become as the youngest, and the leader as one who serves" (Luke 22:26). According to Jesus, leadership is service. However, leading others does not necessarily mean having a **sub**servient attitude or a low self-image. At Victory, we value leadership, and we have seen how God has raised leaders in our church, not because they are smarter, more gifted, or more charismatic, but because they are willing to step out in faith and lead the way in serving the church and the world. When we boldly accept the challenge to lead, we impart faith and courage to those who follow us. Just as quitting is contagious, so it is with bold steps of faith.

When they saw how strong and big their enemies were, the 10 spies were filled with fear. They saw themselves as grasshoppers and their hearts melted. Filipinos look very similar to Malaysians, Indonesians, and many other Asian nationalities. Someone once asked, "How would you identify a Filipino in a large crowd of Asians?"

Answer: "When they move through the crowd, they bow their heads low and repeatedly say, 'Excuse me, excuse me. Pardon me. I'm sorry.'"

The point of the riddle is that most Filipinos are very polite (a good thing), but many have a lower than average self-image (not such a good thing). A low self-image, regardless of nationality, is like a weight that hangs from our necks. As we begin to comprehend who we are in Christ, we begin to emerge from a diminished image of ourselves. That's why I have seen Filipino Christians who are filled with the Holy Spirit and God's Word become as bold as lions.

Pastor Steve, and particularly Pastor Rice, brought with them a unique spirit of faith from their campus ministry at Mississippi State University. They had learned to see one another with eyes of faith—who they were and what they were destined to become in Christ—and they made it a point to encourage one another with that vision. They transplanted that tradition into Victory and instilled the habit of confessing their faith boldly to one another, no matter how young, fearful, or insecure they were.

During the early days, most of the students being saved and discipled in U-Belt were teenagers from the provinces. We typically looked at the floor when someone spoke to us. Most of us were insecure and always apologetic. We exemplified the riddle: "Excuse me, excuse me. Pardon me. I'm sorry." Pastor Steve noticed this right away and did not allow us to think less of ourselves. When Pastor Rice would declare who we are in Christ with such bold faith, I wasn't sure if he believed it for himself or if we were included in that declaration. Breaking that fear and insecurity takes time. Slowly but surely, we realized that he believed it, and we eventually began to see ourselves as God does.

Since those days, that atmosphere of faith has continued in Victory. For new believers, there's nothing more empowering than being seen with eyes of faith and inspired with words of encouragement. That's our job as Victory group leaders.

The author of the epistle to the Hebrews writes: "Let us also lay aside every weight, and sin which clings so closely, and let us run with endurance the race that is set before us" (Hebrews 12:1). Since low self-esteem does no apparent harm to others and often masquerades as humility, we're unaccustomed to categorizing it as a sin. It is, however, a form of doubt and often results in hesitation, fear, and a reluctance to step out in faith. When you think in terms of ultimate outcomes, their grasshopper mentality kept the Israelites from taking hold of God's promise. They died in the wilderness without finishing the race God had set for them. How we see ourselves determines how we take hold of the vision. We must see ourselves with eyes of faith, the way God sees us.

3. Your hesitation causes the vision to fade and the grace to diminish. Have you ever been so moved by a sermon, the presence of God in a meeting, or an experience in your private devotions that caused you to think, *Maybe God is calling me to . . . ?* I understand that people, particularly zealous young believers, can feel compelled to act on every thought that comes to mind. That's not what I'm recommending. However, I know that when people hesitate, procrastinate, or equivocate about answering God's call, Satan often steals the Word right out of their hearts. Whether it's the call to receive the gift of salvation, the call to go into all the world and preach the gospel, or the call to give to a great cause—when they get back around to it, the sense of calling is unclear and the power to say yes has diminished. I've had that experience many times—sensing the leading of the Spirit, but because I did not act on it immediately, the clarity and faith to respond had departed.

Because the spies gave an evil report about giants and fortified cities, the rest of the Israelites lost faith and made travel plans to return to Egypt. Only Joshua and Caleb had the faith to claim God's promise, saying, "Let us go up **at once** and occupy it" (Numbers 13:30). The Israelites' lack of faith displeased God. When the leaders of Israel heard of His intention to have them wander the wilderness for the rest of their lives, they changed their minds and, against Moses' warning and their own fears and doubts, they decided to try and go up into the Promised Land anyway. They were, however, defeated badly because after their initial refusal, God's grace was not with them in the battle (Numbers 14:39-45). Unlike the majority of the Israelites, we must not hesitate to grasp God's call. We must step out in faith.

4. Faith comes with a clear understanding of God's mission. The fundamental mistake that led to the evil report from the 10 spies was that they had misinterpreted the mission. Moses had sent them as spies to see **how**, not **if**, they could conquer their enemies. Only Caleb and Joshua understood the true mission—to plan on how to take the land according to God's promise. After 40 years of wandering in the wilderness and after everyone in that generation had died except for Caleb and Joshua, Moses deputized Joshua to lead the next generation into the Promised Land.

I like to think of Caleb as a faithful partner and pacer for Joshua. At age 85, Caleb came to Joshua and said: "Moses swore on that day, saying, 'Surely the land on which your foot has trodden shall be an inheritance for you and your children forever, because you have wholly followed the Lord my God'" (Joshua 14:9). Caleb had understood the mission, locked in on God's promise, and held on with audacious faith for 40 more years. This is why he is one of my heroes of faith.

Knowing our identity in Christ and Who sustains us, immediately obeying His call, and having audacious faith in understanding God's mission as He does, will help us finish the race that He set before us.

LAST WARNINGS

The central theme in the epistle to the Hebrews is the supremacy of Christ, the better mediator and better high priest in a better temple having offered a better sacrifice. He is the author of a better covenant with a better promise, a better assurance, and a better Sabbath rest. Consequently, the new covenant is far above and beyond every element of the old covenant. The person and work of Jesus Christ did, in fact, fulfill every requirement of the old sacrificial religious system. Because of this, Hebrews is (for Jewish believers in particular) the most extraordinary epistle of the New Testament.

The description of the person and work of Jesus Christ in this epistle is monumental. So are the warnings for Jewish believers who considered retreating from their faith in the face of persecution. In light of the five digressions in the book of Hebrews called "the perils" or "the hazards," the author issued last warnings about the path they were tempted to follow, which can be found in the author's closing remarks (Hebrews 10:19).

Reading the final section in light of this dramatic historical context is quite riveting. I was tempted to simply insert the entire passage. Since, however, I'm only commenting on a few of the verses, I hope you'll give its author's closing remarks a closer look on your own.

1. Resist the temptation to run your race alone. According to commentators, the readers of this epistle were probably part of a small group within the larger church who were separating themselves and contemplating a retreat from their faith in the work Christ had finished. The author encourages them with these words: "Let us hold fast the confession of our hope without wavering, for he who promised is faithful. And let us consider how to stir up one another to love and good works, not neglecting to meet together, as is the habit of some, but encouraging one another, and all the more as you see the Day drawing near" (Hebrews 10:23-25).

Many have experienced what the 16th century monk, Saint John of the Cross, refers to as "the dark night of the soul." In times of emotional and spiritual struggle, even the most devout and faithful are tempted to retreat from fellowship with other believers. This is not a retreat for the sake of spiritual renewal and refreshing of their faith but a retreat from faith and from the presence of the

Spirit. In other words, they become discouraged believers who just don't want to be around anyone trying to cheer them up.

One of my dear friends and *RUN50* supporters is Alfred Romualdez, the former mayor of Tacloban. I believe God put Mayor Romualdez in that position as a man of irrepressible faith, in order to deal with the aftermath of one of the most powerful and destructive storms on record. On November 8, 2013, Typhoon Haiyan (local name Yolanda) devastated the city of Tacloban and left over 10,000 people dead. When the storm had passed, all communications were down, facilities were destroyed, city services were inoperational, and the mayor's staff members were either dead or missing. For the most part, the city's response team in the first few days was just Mayor Alfred—securing supplies, organizing relief operations, and speaking words of faith amidst this most desperate situation. But this was not the same Alfred Romualdez I met before.

After losing a congressional election in 2001, he had determined to withdraw from politics altogether. He also stopped going to church, not wanting to have anything to do with Christians or Christianity. It was "the dark night" of Alfred's soul. Eventually it got so dark that his wife Cristina asked me, "Pastor Ferdie, would you please talk to my husband? I remember you had met him before. I think he would listen to you. He doesn't want to have anything to do with church right now. He's very discouraged."

That's not the first time a wife has called a pastor to solicit help for her husband. I understand that husbands don't often appreciate their wives trying to recruit the pastor's help for some kind of intervention. That would be particularly true for someone like Alfred S. Romualdez, the nephew of Imelda Romualdez Marcos and a member of one of the most powerful political families in the country. And so, I replied, "Okay, Cristina, thank you for calling, but you don't need to call back. I'll take it from here and see if I can find a way to meet him."

I was able to schedule a meeting with him at a coffee shop on a Saturday. Since I had heard that Mr. Romualdez typically shows up early for his appointments, I got there earlier and prepaid at the counter. After some friendly chit-chat, I said, "Sir, we are both busy people, and I don't want to waste your time. I just have two questions I would like to ask you."

"Okay," he said. "What are your questions?"

"First of all, Mr. Romualdez, is Jesus Christ the Lord of your life?"

There was some discussion about what that meant practically, but he agreed eventually, saying, "Yes, Jesus Christ is my Lord."

"Then my second question is this: Would you be willing to be discipled—even if it was by a younger man like me?"

To my astonishment, he enthusiastically said, "Yes." I was trying to stand tall and display confidence, but compared to Mr. Romualdez's place in the world, I must have seemed like a street kid. But there he sat, wanting me to disciple him. What odd and unpredictable things we experience as followers of Christ! I invited him and his wife to a meeting the following day, where I introduced him to Pastor Steve. Over the next 12 weeks, we went through *The Purple Book* together and have remained close friends since.

There was and is a great destiny laid upon Mayor Romualdez's life. Today, he is a man of extraordinary faith and courage, standing against injustice and corruption, championing the cause of the weak and vulnerable. Just think about how different things would have been if he had continued to run his race without men of faith surrounding him and if he had let disappointment and depression get the best of him.

It doesn't matter who you are or where you come from. We all run better when we run with other disciples of Christ.

2. In hard times, comfort and encourage others with the comfort you've received from the Lord. The intended readers of Hebrews were believers who had been running their race for quite some time. No way were they newcomers to the Christian faith. The author wrote, "Remember those earlier days after you had received the light, when you endured in a great conflict full of suffering" (Hebrews 10:32, NIV). Apparently, they had suffered ridicule, public humiliation, and even the plundering of their property. The author commended them for accepting all of this joyfully (Hebrews 11:32-35). However, something much more ominous was coming their way. Some members of the church had been thrown into prison. The author exhorted them to stand firm against their fears. "For you have need of endurance so that when you have done the will of God you may receive what is promised . . . but my righteous one shall live by faith, and if he shrinks back [from the faith], my soul has no pleasure in him" (Hebrews 10:36,38).

One of the most difficult things to do as a pastor or Victory group leader is to give meaningful encouragement to those under your charge, whose faith is being challenged far beyond anything you've ever experienced.

Raissa Laurel was a law student and a member of our worship team at Victory Ortigas. On September 26, 2010, she was waiting for her friends taking the bar exam that day at De La Salle University, when a grenade went off near the campus. This tragedy damaged both her legs so badly that they had to be amputated. When we heard the news, we were all shocked and deeply saddened. One by one, Victory pastors went to visit her in the hospital. I really didn't want to go by myself, so I asked my friend, Cito Beltran, to go with me. I was full of apprehension at the thought of seeing Raissa. I kept asking myself, *What encouragement can I give a young person who lost both her legs and was nearly killed? What do I say to her friends, siblings, parents, and grandparents?* I could easily repeat standard phrases, like, "Have faith, it's all working for the best," or "Thank God you only lost your legs." But even repeating them to myself sounded shallow and superficial. I was expecting a tough and awkward visit.

What do we say to people when the race set before them seems to run straight through the valley of the shadow of death? When we walked into room, I was surprised and relieved to immediately see that Raissa was smiling and in high spirits. Rather than being bitter, she seemed full of hope and gratitude. I thought then that God must surely have a great plan for Raissa's future.

She seemed to have no fear because by faith she sensed that God was with her; like a good shepherd, His rod and staff had comforted her (Psalm 23:4).

I've learned a lot from persevering through the pain, loneliness, and fatigue while running ultramarathons. Far more important are the few things I learned from suffering through the pain of personal disappointments. Whether you are one of those who regularly steps out in faith to lock in on a great vision or if you're more conservative in your ventures into the unknown, sooner or later great challenges that grow your faith will find you.

Raissa continued to run her race, even without any legs. Today, she is a city counselor in San Juan and continues to lead worship regularly at Victory Ortigas. She is another one of my heroes of faith.

The Apostle Paul said in his letter to the church in Colossae that he rejoiced in his sufferings for the sake of the church (Colossians 1:24). He then explained in his letter to the Corinthians how this could happen. It was because of the "God of all comfort, who comforts us in all our affliction, so that we may be able to comfort those who are in any affliction, with the comfort with which we ourselves are comforted by God" (2 Corinthians 1:3,4). Now, I can clearly understand how that works.

3. Have enduring faith in the promises of God. Notice that the author of this epistle didn't refer to his own suffering, endurance, or imprisonments as the Apostle Paul did frequently in his letters. Perhaps these believers were facing challenges that the author had never experienced. And so, rather than appealing to his own experiences, he appealed to the experience of the heroes of the old covenant—almost every one of them. The author framed everything they did in the context of their enduring faith. By faith Noah was warned, Abraham obeyed, Sarah got pregnant, and Moses refused to give up his identity. Many others did not accept release from the torturers and by faith were stoned to death, sawn in two, and so on (Hebrews 11:7-37). The author continued to give 20 more specific examples. He made no reference to the source of their endurance being their commitment, obedience, or knowledge of the Scriptures. In a modern context, the author may have placed value on discovering a particular strength, fine-tuning performance metrics, diets, visioneering, or physical training. However, in his final warning, the author pressed his point and made his case for the one essential spiritual attribute—those who have finished well had been empowered by a living, enduring, and ever-increasing faith. That was their one essential ingredient for victory. It will be for you, as well.

RUN50 CHALLENGE

Most of us have to one degree or another equivocated (hesitated to overcommitting oneself) in response to God's calling. Even those who are listed as the heroes of faith (Noah, Abraham, Jacob, Moses, Gideon, etc.) initially balked at the hurdle of faith in the path laid out for them. However, they eventually locked in on what God had called them to do, and it became for them not a matter of **if**, but **how**, God would enable them to accomplish the vision.

The question and the challenge for us is: to what extent has our equivocation and hesitation become a habit or default mindset? Are we like those who stand on a precipice contemplating a leap of faith, only to find ourselves unable to move, frozen by our doubt and fear? We grow stronger in faith by exercising it. Whether large or small, what step of faith is God calling you to take at this point in your life?

FINISH YOUR RACE

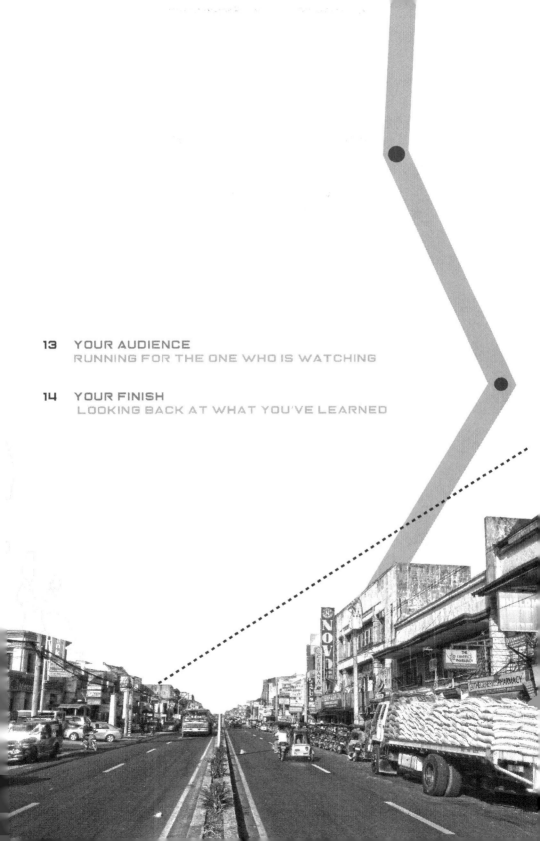

13 YOUR AUDIENCE
    RUNNING FOR THE ONE WHO IS WATCHING

14 YOUR FINISH
    LOOKING BACK AT WHAT YOU'VE LEARNED

13

YOUR AUDIENCE
RUNNING FOR THE ONE WHO IS WATCHING

Don't stop running—your friends are watching!
SPECTATOR SIGN

*Therefore, since **we have so great a cloud of witnesses surrounding us**, let us also lay aside every encumbrance and the sin which so easily entangles us, and let us run with endurance the race that is set before us . . .*
HEBREWS 12:1 (NASB)

Throughout church history, theologians have debated the precise meaning of Hebrews 12:1. The question is: do people in heaven look down on those of us who are still running our races? Some think the passage on the previous page settles the matter—that those who have finished their race are like spectators filling a stadium, cheering for us and watching to see if we, too, will make it to the finish line. Those with that theological perspective refer to Luke 16:28, the story of the rich man in Hades concerned about his brothers, as evidence that departed souls (at least those in Hades) can see events on earth; or to Revelation 6:10 with the martyrs asking God to avenge their deaths.

Both passages indicate that the departed know about things happening on earth, not necessarily that they are spectators glued to the proceedings.

Dr. John Piper, a theologian and Bible teacher, wrote an article in 2017 called, "Can Loved Ones in Heaven Look Down on Me?" He commented:

> I am inclined to think that it does mean that they are watching, partly because of the picture of the race. It is as though the saints finish their marathon at their death. Then they come around and stand on the side of the racetrack and watch us.

On the other hand, there are those who believe the "witnesses" are those whom we emulate as we live our lives today. They note that the word in this passage translated as "witnesses" is the Greek word *martus*, from which comes our English word "martyr." Three times in Hebrews 11, the word *martus* is used to describe the heroes of faith. In Acts 22:20, a reference to the martyrdom of Stephen, Luke writes, "When the blood of Stephen your witness was being shed . . ." Again, the word for witness is *martus*. And so, in the context of the martyrs and heroes of faith in Hebrews 11, those commentators consider a more accurate rendering of Hebrews 12:1 to be, "Therefore, since we are in company of martyrs who kept their faith to the end, let us also run with endurance the race set before us." In other words, the witnesses or martyrs are examples of faith to us, not necessarily spectators. The phrase, "Let us **also** lay aside every weight and run" suggests we are to imitate their endurance and suffering as martyrs, and not just run because someone is watching.

Protestant scholars would caution believers about putting too much emphasis on the heavenly onlookers as those who might help you along the way—such as an appeal to St. Sebastian, the patron saint of athletes, to help them in a run across the Philippines. On the contrary, the author of Hebrews exhorts the readers to fix their eyes on Jesus, the author and perfecter of faith (Hebrews 12:2, NASB). His Holy Spirit is the great Helper and Comforter, as well as our source of spiritual power and boldness.

There are many aspects to the argument. We should keep in mind that the runners, the finish line, and the stadium of onlookers serve as elements of the race metaphor. There may not literally be spectators. Generally speaking, however, most careful theologians like John Piper answer questions about a stadium of heavenly spectators like this: "Maybe so, maybe not. We really don't know for sure." And so with that in mind, let's think for a few moments about the One we know for sure is watching. Here are three takeaways:

1. Empowered by our witnesses: We run better when we are aware that others are watching. It's always empowering to be surrounded by raving fans cheering every step you take. In a basketball game, home-court advantage is hard to measure or understand, but it is without a doubt a real factor. It's not just general cheering that helps you to run your race, it's **who** is cheering that makes all the difference. Fans of an opponent wildly cheering your every mistake and shortcoming won't do much to empower you.

I remember running across the province of Pangasinan in one of my early races. It was very hot, and my energy was almost gone. That's when I heard someone calling to me—"Pastor Ferdie!" The voice came from a car full of church members driven by Pastor CJ Nunag and his wife, Mye, who were on their way to a wedding. They had seen me and stopped the car to cheer me on. It was another one those instances in which I was unsure I would make it to the finish line. It's funny how in so many of those times, something happens or someone shows up to encourage me. In this case, my strength was renewed, and I was able to struggle through to the finish line.

For me, the most empowering fans during *RUN50* were the Real LIFE scholars. On Day 1 of the run, in General Santos City, there was a group of Real LIFE scholars with banners cheering me along near the 50-km mark. As I passed them, they all joined in, running with me until we crossed the finish line. Real LIFE scholars from

Laguna and students from the University of the Philippines Los Baños drove to Alaminos to show their support. In Muntinlupa, Real LIFE scholars from Pasig braved the traffic to run with me. In Cabanatuan City, in front of Central Luzon State University, Real LIFE scholars came with banners and cheered wildly for me as I ran. A group of Real LIFE scholars from Urdaneta City finished their school exam and drove five hours to cheer for a few moments as I ran past them in San Jose, Nueva Ecija. The scholars from Tuguegarao also showed up in the early morning at the hotel lobby to greet me, and then met us again at the finish line at Aparri.

Being aware of spectators definitely has an effect on how you run your race. Much more importantly is the realization that God is watching—not only watching our actions but thoroughly searching out the secrets and deepest motivations of our hearts. No matter your dedication to meditation or introspection, God knows us far more than we can know ourselves, and there is nothing hidden from Him.

I've heard it said that the fear of the Lord is the awareness that He is watching and weighing our every thought and action. That's a pretty scary thought in itself. So it's important to keep in mind that Christ is our great champion, the mediator who continually pleads our case. He is the One whose Spirit empowers, comforts, and encourages us. He is (so to speak) our greatest fan Who is constantly cheering us onto the finish.

There are those who run races not of their choosing but the ones they are compelled to run—the race that has been providentially set before them. They run with great endurance, they run with great faith, and they run in almost complete obscurity. Few, if any, see how they serve, how they give, or how constantly they demonstrate enduring faith. They are simply running for the audience of One.

Though every finisher gets a medal at an ultramarathon, gold, silver, and bronze medals are for the top three finishers. I've never received one of those medals. I'm not that fast; just a persistent plodder. At times, I've wondered as those special awards are passed out how it will be on the last day. Perhaps those who run their race in obscurity, for His eyes only, will be honored at the finish as the greatest of all runners. As Jesus said, "Your Father who sees in secret will reward you openly" (Matthew 6:6, NKJV). I think of my wife, Judy, and her care for our son, Philip. She is one of those heroes who serves only in sight of a very small group of witnesses. She'd probably disagree, but that's how I see her.

2. Empowered by the witnesses who run with you: We run better together. Everyone needs encouragement in the races they're running—everyone! Every Victory group leader, senior pastor, mother and father, student, campus missionary . . . even every young usher as I once was. The writer of Hebrews exhorted his readers in one of his warnings called the Peril of Unbelief, "Take care, brethren, that there not be in any one of you an evil, unbelieving heart that falls away from the living God. **But encourage one another day after day**, as long as it is still called 'Today,' so that none of you will be hardened by the deceitfulness of sin" (Hebrews 3:12-14, NASB). That kind of "day after day" encouragement does not happen automatically. It's the result of an ongoing engagement in a fellowship of encouragement. That's what builds your faith and empowers your race.

From Maasim, Sarangani to Aparri, Cagayan, pacers showed up to join the *RUN50* team. These people took time off from work, drove hundreds of km, and paid for their own accommodations just to run with me for the Real LIFE scholars. Never in my wildest imagination could I have expected this. Knowing I had crew members getting up at 11:00 p.m. every evening to start preparing for the next day's run motivated me to get up and get moving. At times when the road was lonely, the fellowship and camaraderie of purpose was like a shield of faith against boredom and discouragement. When the views were breathtaking, having a pacer to share God's magnificent creation with doubled my sense of appreciation. When the course was difficult and seemingly endless, my pacers and crew gave me extra strength to conquer and finish the race. As noted, I would not have reached the 50-km mark on some days without their encouragement. On several occasions, God used a pacer to remind me why I was running this race at all. When the places were very dangerous, having a pacer (along with some heavily armed escorts) gave me the extra courage to press on. Even now, it's hard to find words to describe how I feel about those who ran with me. *RUN50* would have been impossible without the amazing men and women who escorted me from Sarangani to Aparri. So when, in any context, I say, "We're better together," it has an especially deep meaning for me.

3. Empowered as witnesses to the world: We run better when we are filled with the Holy Spirit. The mission of Every Nation is to honor God by establishing Christ-centered, Spirit-empowered, socially responsible churches and campus ministries in every nation. Together, we are making disciples of all ethnicities by engaging culture and community for Christ, establishing biblical foundations and bringing believers into the church community, equipping them to minister, and empowering them to make disciples. That is our mission and our witness to a watching world.

Victory group leaders are trained to take the gospel into the streets, to their own locality (their offices, homes, and communities), as well as into all vocations—including the government, sports, military, and media. Some are developing a curriculum to rehabilitate drug dependents, others are providing medical assistance to the marginalized, and still others are even bringing the gospel to different tribes that are relocating to cities. Each has their own race to run—the part that God has given them to play.

The disciples were Christ's witnesses to the world—that is, they provided the eyewitness verification of all His mighty words and mighty deeds, including His resurrection. Every record of the apostles' post-resurrection preaching was punctuated with the comment, "And we are witnesses of these things." It doesn't take any special qualification to be a witness; just tell of what you saw and experienced. However, Jesus told His disciples not to go out as witnesses to the world until they were "clothed with power from on high" (Luke 24:49).

To the extent that Victory has been a witness of the resurrected Christ to the Philippines, it has operated with the power of the Holy Spirit. As our vision continues to expand, so does our need to be continuously filled with boldness, wisdom, and the supernatural power of the Holy Spirit.

TO THE HEBREWS

I've talked about championing the cause of those in great need by personally identifying with their pain, sufferings, or struggles. In the closing remarks to this group of Jewish believers, the writer urged them to embrace and identify both with the sufferings of Christ, and with the sufferings of those who have already been thrown into prison. Hebrews 13:3 (NIV) says, "Continue to remember those in prison as if you were **together with them in prison**, and those who are mistreated **as if you yourselves were suffering**." And Hebrews 13:12 (NIV) continues, "Let us, then, go to [Christ] outside the camp, **bearing the disgrace he bore**."

It must have been a fearful thing to come forward and associate oneself with one of these unfortunate believers who had been imprisoned under conditions we can only imagine. In many places around the world, identifying yourself with a prisoner immediately puts you under suspicion and might lead you to the same fate. Boldly associating yourself with Christ could eventually provoke authorities to do with you what they did to Him. It was fear of association with Christ that caused Peter to deny Him three times. Apparently, professing Christ openly and boldly had become an issue for those whose faith was wavering. Consequently, one of the closing remarks was: "Let us continually offer to God a sacrifice of praise—the fruit of lips that **openly profess** his name" (Hebrews 13:15, NIV).

Nicodemus boldly associated with the crucified Savior. He was not mentioned among the heroes of faith in Hebrews 11, but I think he could have been in that number. It would have read something like this: "By faith, Nicodemus went to Pilate, claimed the body of Jesus, and buried Him in a tomb." For anyone who has ever taken a bold stand for Christ, risking the consequences of identifying with Him, old Nicodemus could be your hero, too.

RUN50 CHALLENGE

We run better when we're filled with the Holy Spirit. Even after being baptized with the Holy Spirit, we can still be filled again with Him. Several times in the Acts of the Apostles, Luke records that they were filled with the Holy Spirit again (Acts 4:8,31; 13:9,52). People typically testify to being filled with the Holy Spirit at a particular point in time. The Apostle Paul wrote to the church in Ephesus: "Do not be drunk with wine... but be filled [literally 'be being filled'] with the Spirit" (Ephesians 5:18).

As is often the case with historical accounts, being filled with the Holy Spirit can be interpreted in several ways. Were these encounters with the Holy Spirit to be thought of as subsequent baptisms in the Spirit, as refilling, or as empowerment for the need of the moment? It's not so much about what we call these encounters; instead, it is about our sense of dependency on Him and the reality of being empowered by the Holy Spirit. To be the witnesses to the watching world as God has called us to be, we need to ask, seek, and receive the filling of the Holy Spirit continually. And so, the challenge is to be filled with His power, boldness, and joy, over and over and over again.

We run better together. With regard to the spiritual race, who are your pacers? Who is running with you? Who is challenging you, telling you that you've gone off-course, encouraging you to do your best, and reminding you of your purpose and calling? If you're not joined together with some other great runners, it's hard to keep pace.

We run better when we are running for the One who we know is watching. The Holy Spirit is quite persistent in uncovering and bringing to light secret motives that rule in the hearts of Christ's servants. And nothing will challenge the motives of our hearts quite like running a race, living a life, or serving the Lord in relative obscurity. It may be that such a lonely race is, in fact, part of a divine plan. Consequently, it's not hard to imagine that the greatest of all His servants are those of whom few, if any, have ever heard.

Sometimes, in a very different way, the Lord tests and proves the hearts of His servants by allowing them to prosper and become so productive that the heads of all spectators are turned to focus on what they and their team are doing. There are lots of us in both categories—the runners of obscurity and runners of note. Enough has happened through Victory that many may fit into the renowned category—the "celebrated servants of the Lord." But how do we treat servants in the Body of Christ who have (so to speak) "fished all night and caught nothing?" More importantly than how we treat them (for we can feign humility and enthusiasm), how do we truly esteem them in our hearts?

The Scriptures say, "'Everyone to whom much was given, of him much will be required, and from him to whom they entrusted much, they will demand the more'" (Luke 12:48). Many people read that verse and immediately conclude that those of us entrusted with a great stewardship are required to work more than the rest. I think a better understanding of the Lord's parable is not simply that we are required to **do more** but that we are required to **be more**. And so, whether your labors are highly celebrated or rarely noticed, our challenge is to run our races with an awareness of the audience of the One Great Spectator.

14

YOUR FINISH
LOOKING BACK AT WHAT YOU'VE LEARNED

I have no formula for winning the race. Everyone runs in her own way or his own way. And where does the power come from to see the race to its end? From within. Jesus said, "Behold, the Kingdom of God is within you. If with all your hearts, you truly seek me, you shall ever surely find me." If you commit yourself to the love of Christ, then that is how you run a straight race.

ERIC LIDDELL
1924 Paris Olympics, Gold Medalist, 400 m
Missionary to China

*I have fought the good fight, **I have finished the race**, I have kept the faith. Henceforth there is laid up for me the crown of righteousness, which the Lord, the righteous judge, will award to me on that day, and not only to me but also to all who have loved his appearing.*

2 TIMOTHY 4:7,8

In the introduction to the epistle to the Hebrews, the writer described Jesus Christ sitting down after finishing His race. "After making purification for sins, he **sat down** at the right hand of the Majesty on high, having become as much superior to angels as the name he has inherited is more excellent than theirs" (Hebrews 1:3,4). After partaking of the sour wine while hanging on the cross (a fulfillment of Psalm 69:21), Jesus said, "'**It is finished**,' and he bowed his head and gave up his spirit" (John 19:30).

The writer of Hebrews diverts slightly from the metaphor of a runner's discipline to comment on the Lord's discipline (Hebrews 12:5-11). It's one thing to "**discipline yourself** for the purpose of godliness" (1 Timothy 4:7, NASB), quite another to say, "**He disciplines us** for our good, that we may share his holiness" (Hebrews 12:10, NASB)—two very different things; two very different actors. Disciplining yourself is a constant battle with your own comfort, your own desire to fall back, or even the temptation to quit the race. On the other hand, being disciplined by the Lord is a battle of faith. My experience is that this is the much tougher battle, the much greater challenge. The two battles, however, are not unrelated. In times of our greatest disillusionment, when we ask, "God, how could you let this happen?" it is our rule of discipline (such as practicing spiritual disciplines) that gets us through.

The writer's final warning is in the last few verses: "See to it that no one comes short of the grace of God; that no root of bitterness springing up causes trouble, and by it many be defiled" (Hebrews 12:15, NASB). We don't know the exact situation he was referring to, but it's not hard to imagine. Amid intense difficulty and disillusionment, the natural tendency is to start pointing fingers—blaming leaders, blaming competitors, or blaming God for the difficulty of the race set before you. Bitterness is like cancer. It spreads and metastasizes through your body. Your troubles tend to multiply because bitterness leads to all kinds of bad decisions. In the end, it destroys you.

In his final word to the recipients of his letter, the author writes, "See that you do not refuse him who is speaking. For if they did not escape when they refused him who warned them on earth, much less will we escape if we reject him who warns from heaven" (Hebrews 12:25). So, what happened? Did these individuals, having acknowledged their faith in the person and work of Jesus Christ, backslide into apostasy? It's impossible to say. We do know that the author of the epistle, whoever he was, made a most compelling case. If, in fact, the letters were addressed and delivered to the leaders of this small group, I believe that at least some of them must have finished their race with their faith intact. If not, the epistle to the Hebrews might not have survived.

FINAL TAKEAWAYS FROM *RUN50*

Before, during, and after *RUN50*, I've thought a lot about the spiritual race we're all running together. Below are a few things to consider:

1. **Your Competition**

    It's very hard in the beginning to understand that the whole idea is not to beat the other runners. Eventually you learn that the competition is against the little voice inside you that wants you to quit.

    Dr. George Sheehan (1918-1993)
Medical Editor of *Runner's World* Magazine
World's First Sub-Five-Minute Mile by a 50-year-old

    . . . they [the disciples of Jesus] had argued with one another about who was the greatest.

    Mark 9:34

Have you ever noticed that there's something different about Christian leaders who've come to realize that they're running an ultramarathon rather than a 100-m dash? They're less likely to compare their ministries to others. They don't esteem other runners by the size of their churches. They're far more likely to help and encourage those other runners along the way.

For ultramarathoners, other competitors are usually not the primary focus. We're racing against our own limitations and desire to quit. It's not about how fast one runs but if he or she finishes the race. The best finisher in the *160-km Bataan Death March* in 2012 was Juny Rex Carreon (21:07:56). In *Aesop's Fables*, there is a story about a race between the tortoise and the hare. "Slow and steady wins the race," says the tortoise. Well, I've never actually won a sanctioned race or any ultramarathon I've ever entered. But slow and steady did enable me to finish—32nd out of the 53 who started the race with a time of 28:44:46, almost five hours behind the top female runner, Keshia Fule (23:56:31).

In 2013, I met Jorell Paringit, a member of Victory Tuguegarao, while he was running his first *160-km Bataan Death March*. As we were running, I noticed Jorrel was not properly covered for the heat of the sun. Remembering how I struggled with the heat and sunburn in past races, I offered him my spare cap with a nape cover. Then I noticed that his crew was positioned too far from him. So when we stopped, I offered my water, food, and other runner's supplies. When he needed to rest, I waited for him.

It is common practice for ultramarathoners to offer help to fellow runners. That's especially true for Filipinos—it is our custom. Runners stopping to drink or eat will say *"kain po tayo"* (let's eat) to their fellow runner. I've seen that happen in all the ultramarathon races I've joined.

Runners competing in the 100-m sprint never have much sympathy for their competitors or think of helping them along the way. It's all about winning and placing. However, the farther you go, the more your race becomes a test of endurance and the more camaraderie there is among the runners. We are, in a sense, all cheering for one another. Ultramarathoners are a lot like ultra-mountain climbers. They seem to be more like comrades than competitors, especially in difficult times.

That's reminiscent of a less-than-stellar moment among some of Jesus' closest disciples.

"And they came to Capernaum. And when he was in the house he asked them, 'What were you discussing on the way?' But they kept silent, for on the way they had argued with one another about who was the greatest" (Mark 9:33,34).

James and John were the ones who tried to force Jesus into an agreement to promote them to a position, sitting to the right and to the left of Jesus when He came into His kingdom. Clearly, they were operating with a very short-term perspective regarding Christ and His kingdom—as a sprint rather than a marathon. What the Gospel of Mark describes in the immediately following verses is predictable.

> John said to him, "Teacher, we saw someone casting out demons in your name, and we tried to stop him, because he was not following us." But Jesus said, "Do not stop him, for no one who does a mighty work in my name will be

able soon afterward to speak evil of me. For the one who is not against us is for us."

Mark 9:38-40

Founding leaders of Victory, particularly Pastors Steve and Rice, Al Manamtam, Tom Bouvier, and others, set a tone of humility that the rest of us have followed. When any of us have wandered from that ideal or started comparing ourselves to one another or our ministry to someone else's, we've embarrassed ourselves just as those first disciples did who were rebuked by the Lord for having a wrong spirit. Every believer, leader, and church runs their own race. If you see it as a short run, you'll be as competitive and petty as the early disciples in that instance. If you have a long-distance perspective, you might be gracious enough to realize that we're all running together as a team.

2. **Your Crown**

Gold medals aren't really made of gold. They're made of sweat, determination, and a hard-to-find alloy called guts.

Dan Gable
1972 Munich Olympics, Wrestler, Gold Medalist

And when the chief Shepherd appears, you will receive the unfading crown of glory.

1 Peter 5:4

In most of the New Testament books, the "crown of life" is referenced repeatedly. It's difficult to fully explain in a few words, so I'll just outline what is implied by the New Testament writers.

The crown is not your good works; it's made up of the people you have served. The Apostle Paul posed a rhetorical question to the saints in Thessalonica: "For what is hope, our joy, or the crown in which we will glory in the presence of our Lord Jesus when he comes? **Is it not you?**" (1 Thessalonians 2:19, NIV). Those you bring with you constitute your reward or your crown at the coming of Christ.

We present those who have been entrusted to our stewardship as an offering to Christ at His coming. The Apostle Paul's expectation seemed to be that he would present the Gentiles to Christ as an offering. "Because of the grace that was given me from God, to be a minister of Christ Jesus to the Gentiles, ministering as a priest the gospel of God, so that my offering of the Gentiles may become acceptable, sanctified by the Holy Spirit" (Romans 15:15,16, NASB). It follows that the ministry entrusted to you as a stewardship—that is, those you have engaged, equipped, established, and empowered with the gospel, will be the offering that you too will present to Christ at His coming.

Those who are faithful in the spiritual care of others will receive crowns of glory that last for all eternity. Disciplining, mentoring, and serving the saints is a high calling and for those who perform these duties in the character of the Chief Shepherd, the reward will be unimaginable. Peter, the great apostle, echoed what the Apostle Paul said about his stewardship, the crown of glory, and the Lord's coming: "Shepherd the flock of God that is among you, exercising oversight, not under compulsion, but willingly, as God would have you; not for shameful gain, but eagerly; not domineering over those in **your charge**, but being examples to the flock. And when the **chief Shepherd appears, you will receive the unfading crown of glory**" (1 Peter 5:2-4).

The crown of life, or the "crown of unfading glory" is not just for those who run well and finish well. According to the Apostles Paul and Peter, there seems to be a special crowning for those who are committed to making disciples and caring for the saints.

3. **Your Champion-ship**

   Champions aren't made in gyms. Champions are made from something they have deep inside them—a desire, a dream, a vision. They have to have the skill, and the will. But the will must be stronger than the skill.

   Muhammad Ali
World Champion Boxer

   In the heavens God has pitched a tent for the sun. It is like a bridegroom coming out of his chamber, like a champion rejoicing to run his course.

   Psalm 19:4,5 (NIV)

   In earlier chapters I talked about becoming a champion—that is, championing the cause of those in need, just as Jesus Christ became our "Savior and Champion" (Isaiah 19:20, NASB). There seems to be several unfolding layers of champion-ship, which I outlined in chapter 9.

Running to raise funds for others. That is, indeed, a great thing to do. If you're going to run, you might as well run for something. Unbelievers do that as much as Christians. Every race seems to be a fundraiser for something or somebody. Of course, that doesn't mean all runners have a philanthropic intent or think of themselves as championing the cause of those in need. Many are just participants who are, incidentally, supporting a cause.

Identifying so deeply with those you are called to serve that your championship becomes a personal passion. One of my stated purposes of *RUN50* was for my son, Philip. I wasn't raising funds for my son. I was running in his place because of my identification with him. I identify with him in his happy times and in his sufferings—with his personal challenges and with his personal victories.

I was also running to raise money for Real LIFE scholars. I identify with their hopes and dreams as well as the seemingly impossible hill many children in the Philippines have to climb. I think about my father, who fled the Japanese occupation of the Visayas. He was a great man and a great father, but he was also a poor farmer who never learned to read or write. It was only because of my mother and my aunt's vision, as well as their financial sacrifices, that my sisters and I were the first in my extended family to obtain college degrees. It is often difficult for Filipino families to climb out of poverty without somebody becoming their champion.

Understanding your stewardship from God in terms of champion-ship. In the words of the Apostle Paul, "I became a minister according to the stewardship from God that was **given to me for you**" (Colossians 1:25). Raising money on behalf of others is a good thing to do. Deeply identifying with them and their need is an even greater thing. But standing in the gap for a particular group of people is a very high calling. It's one that exemplifies the ministry of Christ who gave Himself up for us.

Taking on a champion-ship of the greatest eternal significance. Championing the cause of those in need is not just a social program or community service project to better the nation or community. Jesus so identified with those in need that He said to His disciples concerning those who were hungry, thirsty, naked, sick, or aliens in the land, "As you have done it to the least of these, you have **done it to me**" (Matthew 25:40, AKJV). As the *RUN50* team raised money for Real LIFE scholars, we felt like Jesus was saying, "You did it for Me."

Saul of Tarsus felt the terrible sting of Christ's identification with the saints when the risen Christ spoke to him and said, "Saul, Saul. Why are you **persecuting me**?" (Acts 9:4; 22:7,8; 26:14). For what Saul was doing to the saints, Jesus took personally. He considered it as being done to Him.

On the other hand, for those who serve the saints, Hebrews 6:10 (NASB) says, "God is not unjust so as to forget your work and the love which you have shown **toward His name**, in having ministered and in still ministering to the saints."

4. **Your Completion**

I'd made it this far and refused to give up because all my life I had always finished the race.

Louis Zamperini
1936 Berlin Olympics, 5000 m
Subject of the book and movie, *Unbroken*

I consider my life worth nothing to me; my only aim is to finish the race and complete the task the Lord Jesus has given me—the task of testifying to the good news of God's grace.

Acts 20:24 (NIV)

During the last week of *RUN50*, I was running through the Northeastern Luzon provinces of Nueva Vizcaya, Isabela, and Cagayan. On Sunday, October 18, we heard that tropical storm Koppu (local name Lando) was headed for Baguio City on the day of my run through the Dalton Pass promising to bring much rain and wind to Nueva Vizcaya. Teams from Victory Nueva Vizcaya and Isabela, led by Pastor Rommar Flores and Pastor Jojo Vaquilar, were scheduled to join me. However, the threatening weather forced us to consider a postponement. I'd endured a lot of pain and exhaustion to stay on schedule and wasn't inclined to take a day off at the very end. We left the hotel at around 11:00 p.m. to make our way to back to where we had ended the previous day. I was surprised that there was not even a drop of rain. I had been told that we would be running through the eye of the storm, though we found out later that it was over Baguio. By the time we arrived at our starting point, it was like running through a typhoon. The winds and rain were relentless. We heard later that the downpour that day caused many landslides and floods. After we made our way through Dalton Pass, it was closed to all vehicles. I am forever thankful to the brave men and women who ran with me and served as my crew that day. They did not abandon me even though it was dangerous.

After the Sunday rest and the run through Dalton Pass, we continued north through the province of Isabela where we were warmly welcomed by residents, attendees from church, and Real LIFE scholars. Along the road, I saw two elderly men. As I approached, they introduced themselves as pastors of a Pentecostal church in one of the barrios. They had heard about our *RUN50* route through their province and had walked to see me. They gave me some crackers and an envelope containing their contribution to Real LIFE.

Experiences like this throughout *RUN50* made my heart swell with thankfulness for this opportunity to witness how God can touch people's lives. I took time after the day's run to pray for the town officials and university students, ending the day with Pastors Jojo Vaquilar, Jude Lingan, and Jay Medrano, and their leaders.

I continued my run to Tuguegarao City where Pastor Ross Resuello and his team managed to round up the whole town to welcome the Running Pastor. There was music, drums, and a lot of cheering. It was a great celebration. The mayor of the city joined me in running for a few km. I boldly preached the gospel, prayed for the city officials, and pronounced a blessing for the whole city. On October 25, a Sunday, Pastor Ross asked me to preach in the morning service at Victory Tuguegarao.

After the service, we headed back to the hotel to have lunch with Pastor Ross, his family, and some staff members. While we were having lunch, to my complete surprise, Pastors Steve and Jun Escosar walked in. My eyes filled with tears when I saw them. It was like my father and brother showing up for my school graduation. My daughter, Elle, and my nephew, Tim, also arrived from Manila to join me on the last day of *RUN50*.

After a brief time of fellowship and storytelling, I went to my room to rest. At 11:00 p.m., as had been my tradition for the last 43 run days, I woke up and started preparing for the final day's run. I felt very excited about the day that would mark the end and fulfillment of my dream. I kept thinking to myself, *Could it be that I am about to complete the challenge that I had locked in on so many years ago? But here it is, the last day of* RUN50!

I joined the team that had assembled at the hotel lobby at about 12:00 a.m. As I looked around, I saw all these people who had made the effort to join me—my daughter and nephew; my pacers Junn Besana, Jorell Paringit, Jonathan Navalta, and Geraldine Santiago; Real LIFE scholars; and the Victory Tuguegarao staff members. Everyone seemed to feel the excitement of finishing the race. "This is it!" we kept saying to one another.

We started the run at 2:00 a.m. It was drizzling and cool, which is great weather for runners. It was a fun run—no more scorching heat, pain with every step, or torturous mountains to climb. I felt enthused and empowered. I was finishing strong.

At the break of dawn, we were getting close to the town of Aparri. Later in the morning, we were beginning to pass people lined up on the side of the streets—pastors from the provinces, policemen, members from our Victory churches in the north, and even people from our church in Manila all came out to cheer us onto the end. When I saw the 00-km mark on the side of the street, I knew that I was in Aparri, my final destination. I stopped and stood still for a few moments and looked around for my daughter. When I finally saw her, we joined hands and ran together toward the beach.

As I approached the marked finish line, I couldn't help but think, *This is exactly how I imagined it would be.* Since the first day in Maasim, Sarangani, I'd been visualizing crossing the finish line in Aparri. This mental picture helped me endure difficulties and continue pressing forward, not giving into the temptation to quit.

I crossed the finish line with my daughter by my side and broke through the ribbon Pastor Ross and his team had prepared. Elle was crying; I was jubilant.

We went down to the beach to get water from the northern tip of the Philippines. A lone fisherman seated on top of the breakwaters was so surprised at the great throng of people that had suddenly appeared. I asked him if I could borrow his pail to scoop up some ocean water. There was, of course, no finishing medal for *RUN50*. My only trophies are the two little bottles of ocean water, one from the beginning of my run in Maasim, Sarangani, and one from Aparri, Cagayan, where I finished my race.

The mayor of Aparri, Dr. Shalimar Tumaru, set up a stage where she gathered all her officials and staff to welcome us to her province. People were cheering and everyone was celebrating. It was a big fiesta. We were introduced, and I was given a chance to speak. And speak I did, from the Apostle Paul's letter to Timothy.

> I urge that supplications, prayers, intercessions, and thanksgivings be made for all people, for kings and all who are in high positions, that we may lead a peaceful and quiet life, godly and dignified in every way. This is good, and it is pleasing in the sight of God our Savior, who desires all people to be saved and to come to the knowledge of the truth.
> 1 Timothy 2:1-4

I preached the gospel with great fervency to all who were there and made an altar call, giving people a chance to respond to the grace found in the gospel. Many people, including the mayor, raised their hands, and I led them in prayer. After my sermon and invitation to follow Christ, I prayed a prayer of blessing for the mayor and her officials and for the town of Aparri. When all this was done, we were led to some tents where food had been prepared for everyone. It was one big boodle fight!

After our hearty breakfast, I went back to the old pier where a concrete landing extended to the ocean. I walked on the landing and, facing the ocean, I raised both hands and gave glory to God Who had called me to champion the cause of those in need and empowered me to run for those who could not run themselves.

RUN50 **CHALLENGE**

From the beginning of *RUN50* at Maasim, Sarangani to the finish line at Aparri, I was deeply inspired every time Real LIFE scholars would show up. Though the Philippines is known for its poverty, one way to break the cycle is through education. But for that to happen, someone has to step into the lives of the children as their champion. And the Real LIFE Foundation is doing just that. Truly, we can make a big difference if we join together to help one kid at a time.

Most of us don't live under the threat of assassination or martyrdom. However, we are all martyrs in the sense that we are witnesses. As noted in chapter 13, the Greek word *martus* is translated in Hebrews 12:1 and other verses as "witnesses." "Since we are surrounded by such a great cloud of **martyrs**, let us run with endurance the race set before us, fixing our eyes on Jesus."

To press the point a little further about our focus and our calling to follow Christ as "martyr-witnesses," the Apostle Paul wrote to the Colossian church, "Set your minds on things that are above, not on things that are on earth. For **you have died**, and your life is hidden with Christ in God" (Colossians 3:2,3). And again, the words of Jesus Himself: "If anyone would come after me, let him deny himself and **take up his cross** (the instrument of crucifixion) **daily** and follow me. For whoever would save his life will lose it, but whoever **loses his life for my sake** will save it" (Luke 9:23,24). And so, for the apostles, for the modern-day disciples, and even (and especially) for Victory group leaders, we are to consider ourselves as dead men walking. And in the context of the race set before us—as dead men and women running.

When runners are close to the completion of their life's race, they tend to evaluate the relative meaning or meaninglessness of their lives. The question and the *RUN50* challenge is this: by what measure do you think about such things? Is it the accumulation of money, fame, and power? How about a long and healthy life with lots of successful children and grandchildren? Perhaps, it's a large church with many disciples bearing fruit a hundredfold. Nothing is intrinsically wrong with any of those measurements, except they all place a value on the meaningfulness of your race based on numbers. But what about those who devote their lives to championing the cause of a special-needs child or supporting the educational opportunities for a few of the millions of underprivileged kids in the Philippines? How about Victory group leaders who focus on making disciples one by one, never aspiring positions or promotions?

Have you felt that the race set before you was a waste because it didn't result in big numbers? Have you ever been told by friends or relatives that you're wasting your life by following hard after Christ? Even Christ's closest disciples initially viewed His suffering and crucifixion as a terrific waste. However, fixing our eyes intently on the risen Jesus Christ who endured the cross and despised the shame of it all (Hebrews 12:1,2) tends to change our perspective.

A meaningful life is not always about the pursuit of big numbers. Focusing on His victory empowers us to run with endurance and finish strong.

Epilogue

Tomorrow is another day, and there will be another battle.

SEBASTIAN COE
1980 Moscow Olympics, **Gold Medalist, 1500 m**
1984 Los Angeles Olympics, **Gold Medalist, 1500 m**

Not that I have already obtained it or have already become perfect, but I press on so that I may lay hold of that for which also I was laid hold of by Christ Jesus. Brethren, I do not regard myself as having laid hold of it yet; but one thing I do: forgetting what lies behind and reaching forward to what lies ahead, I press on toward the goal for the prize of the upward call of God in Christ Jesus.

PHILIPPIANS 3:12-14 (NASB)

After running 50 km a day, six days a week for over seven weeks, my body had gotten used to it, and I didn't want to stop too abruptly. So, the day after the finish of *RUN50*, I ran 20 km to Callao Cave by myself. Then I went back to the hotel, ate my breakfast, and rested the whole day. It's what ultramarathoners call a "recovery run."

I thought about what Coach Salazar had told me in the early days of training for *RUN50*. "See those older guys on the track?" He said, "They walk instead of run because they started late. But you're a lifetime runner, and you're not going to be like that, Ferdie. My goal for you is that you'll still be running well into your 70s."

I am now 52 years old and not done with running, championing the cause of those in need, or raising funds for Real LIFE scholars. By the time this book is published, I will have completed a 550-km run around the island of Cebu in November 2017. As I write this book, the governor has already shown excitement about the idea and has met with all the mayors to get them on board. We have other runs planned for Panay Island in 2018, another major island in 2019, and possibly a run across Palawan in 2020—one of the longest of the Philippine islands. I'll be 60 years old in 2025 and have something really big in mind to celebrate it with.

RUN50 CHALLENGE

As I was nearing the end of *RUN50*, I began thinking about all the things we had gone through—rebel-controlled areas in Mindanao on a very painful ankle and Leyte during a tsunami warning. We had been on some of the most beautiful and mountainous roads and through Dalton Pass amidst the deluge of storm Koppu (local name Lando). I thought about the six people who had run across the Philippines before me and felt an uncommon bond with them. I'm now number seven. It's the same kind of camaraderie I feel with the friends who have been running with me for many years and with my brothers and sisters—those with whom I am running a spiritual race.

And I thought about one of my heroes of faith, Caleb the son of Jephunneh, who, along with Joshua and ten others, was sent as a spy into the Promised Land to see how it could be taken. The evil report of the ten faithless and fearful spies so thoroughly infected the nation of Israel that they began to make plans *en masse* to return to their slavery in Egypt. As a result, they were condemned to wandering in the wilderness for 40 years, one year for each of the 40 days it took them to arrive at the edge of God's promise. That entire generation spent the rest of their lives wandering around in the wilderness and eventually died there. Only Joshua and Caleb remained. Moses made a promise to Caleb: "Surely the land on which your foot has trodden shall be an inheritance for you and your children forever because you have wholly followed the Lord my God" (Joshua 14:9). And Caleb held onto that promise for 45 years.

This is a very familiar story, and you all know it well. I'm reminding you of it again to make one final point; to answer one final question. What is it that empowers some people to be as full of faith and vision, to be as passionate for Christ and dedicated to His mission, and to run with as much endurance at the end of their race as they did at the beginning? This is what Caleb said about himself:

> "And now, behold, the Lord has kept me alive, just as he said, these forty-five years since the time that the Lord spoke this word to Moses, while Israel walked in the wilderness.

> And now, behold, I am this day eighty-five years old. I am still as strong today as I was in the day that Moses sent me; my strength now is as my strength was then, for war and for going and coming. So now give me this hill country of which the Lord spoke on that day . . ."
>
> Joshua 14:10-12

Caleb was a multigenerational man. More importantly, he had a multigenerational vision for the people he was called to lead and for his own life. It's what kept faith and passion burning inside him through the times when others were fading and retiring. Young men and women naturally tend to have a perspective focused on the near or immediate future. I'm committed to lead with the next generation and the generation after that and the generation after that. My hope and my intention is to continue preaching the gospel, making disciples, and training leaders until they put me in the ground. And if, in my later days, my audience and influence shrinks to only a few, my vision is to impart to them the same passion for Christ I've tried to share with Victory group leaders and members in these present times. As is written on the gravestone of the great missionary and passionate disciple, William Borden: "No reserves. No retreat. No regrets!"

> Therefore, since we are surrounded by so great a cloud of witnesses, let us also lay aside every weight, and sin which clings so closely, and let us run with endurance the race that is set before us . . .
>
> Hebrews 12:1

References

Carroll, Lewis. (1865) 1998. *Alice's Adventures in Wonderland.* Chicago, IL: VolumeOne Publishing.

Collins, Jim, and Morton T. Hansen. 2011. *Great by Choice: Uncertainty, Chaos, and Luck—Why Some Thrive despite Them All.* NY: HarperCollins Publishers.

Elliot, Elisabeth. 1992. *The Shaping of a Christian Family: How My Parents Nurtured My Faith.* Grand Rapids, MI: Fleming H. Revell.

Encyclopaedia Britannica Online, s.v. "Bataan Death March," accessed August 31, 2017, https://www.britannica.com/event/Bataan-Death-March.

Grudem, Wayne. 1995. "Perseverance of the Saints: A Case Study from Hebrews 6:4-6 and the Other Warning Passages of Hebrews." Vol. 1 of *The Grace of God, the Bondage of the Will: Biblical and Practical Perspectives on Calvinism,* edited by Thomas R. Schreiner and Bruce A. Ware, 133-182. Grand Rapids, MI: Baker.

Murrell, Steve. 2011. *WikiChurch: Making Discipleship Engaging, Empowering, & Viral.* Lake Mary, FL: Charisma House.

Murrell, Steve. 2013. *100 Years from Now: Sustaining a Movement for Generations.* Nashville, TN: Dunham Books.

Oxford Dictionaries, s.v. "equivocation," accessed August 31, 2017, https://en.oxforddictionaries.com/definition/equivocation.

Piper, John. 2017. "Can Loved Ones in Heaven Look Down on Me?" *Ask Pastor John* 995 (January 2017). Accessed August 31, 2017, https://www.desiringgod.org/interviews/can-loved-ones-in-heaven-look-down-on-me.

About the Author

Ferdie Cabiling is the director of Victory, one church with multiple locations in Metro Manila.

A preacher and an evangelist who can craft sermon notes on the back of receipts, Ferdie is also an avid ultramarathoner known for his uncanny ability to nap while running. He has completed four marathons and ten ultramarathons, including the infamous *160-km Bataan Death March*, twice. In 2015, he ran 2,180 km across the Philippines in less than 50 days at the age of 50 to raise awareness and funds for the scholars of the Real LIFE Foundation.

In 2016, Ferdie was ordained a bishop of Victory as he continues to oversee the leadership and growth of Victory in Metro Manila.

Ferdie holds a Bachelor of Science degree in Civil Engineering from Adamson University. He is currently pursuing a Master's degree in Intercultural Studies, focused on Church Planting, at the Asbury Theological Seminary. He and his wife Judy have two children, Elizabeth and John Philip, and have been married for over twenty-six years.

Made in the USA
Columbia, SC
03 July 2019